RETL....

BOMB ALLEY

1982

THE FALKLANDS DECEPTION

PAUL CARDIN

FOREWORD

Back in the safety of her London bunker, Margaret Thatcher [1] surrounded herself with men. [2] "But", we were reassured, "she's the one wearing the trousers."

8,000 miles away, we also wore trousers, but we risked our lives on the front line, bailing Thatcher out.

———— ✦✦✦✦ ————

The year 2022 marks the 40th Anniversary of the Falklands Conflict. 1982 was itself the 40th anniversary of the two Battles of El Alamein, where British soldiers and their allies risked their lives to push back Rommel, keep control over the operation of the Suez Canal and influence over the oil fields of the Middle East. As a nation, our need to preserve strategic waterways and far-flung resources beneath a banner of patriotism and service of country had been well established.

———— ✦✦✦✦ ————

[1] https://en.wikipedia.org/wiki/First_Thatcher_ministry
[2] https://www.youtube.com/watch?v=ThkVqCYdR0Y

Here's a link to my original [3] Falklands War Diary, handwritten on location [password: 1982345654321982].

I put pen to paper in the MCO (Main Communications Office) of HMS Yarmouth in between Argentine air raids, calls to action stations, false alarms, naval gunfire support bombardments and rescue missions.

Like a sudden change in the weather, it felt natural to be on a warship in harbour one day and sailing to a far-off place the next. We were young Royal Navy volunteers after all and like freshly fallen autumn leaves settling on a river, we were captured and carried along on the stream. It didn't matter where we ended up. We had no choice in our destination.

These trials were brief, gruelling at times, but life-affirming. The sometimes precious, sometimes crushing wisdoms gained would endure for the rest of our lives.

I remember how, at the HMS Mercury training base in Petersfield, Hampshire, during the scorching summer of 1976, my overriding concern was; "Would the milkman visit soon, dishing out ice cold drinks?" By spring 1982, this had changed to; "Would an Exocet missile visit soon, dishing out death?"

So that year, it hit us like a sledgehammer that wars kill, maim, or mentally damage their participants, giving few a second chance. With this to the forefront of our minds, we were hyper-vigilant as we watched peace proposals being ignored,

---

[3]   https://wirralinittogether.blog/2021/10/25/paul-cardin-bomb-alley-1982-the-falklands-deception-my-falklands-war-diary/

viewed as worthless, treated with contempt, or used cynically as tools to distract the British or Argentine public.

I should state at the outset, here I am with a book out, one that's stuffed with facts and opinions. Much of the content here isn't so hard and fast and will be questionable – which goes with the territory – and it won't be easy for readers to discern truth. Upon completing the book, please feel free to go with your own gut feeling and to reach your own verdict on the authenticity of the content.

In the diary, you will see how I reported the events unfolding around me quickly, objectively and without jotting down any private thoughts. I didn't venture into day-to-day life on the ship or the interactions between the crew because I hadn't the time, and post-conflict, hadn't the inclination!

Within the 1982 diary text I've enlarged upon the old content by including links to online news articles, websites, and videos. Some thoughts giving more context are in italics. These are here to help you if you're new to the subject, or if not, to refresh your memory on these rapidly receding events. Some photos are included. Contemporary thoughts of mine were added in 2021. The content is now being published as an eBook and as a printed book. Hyperlinks are included as numbered footnotes.

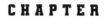

CHAPTER

1

ABOUT THE MAN

Paul Cardin - August 2020

***Paul Cardin was born in Wallasey**, Wirral, Merseyside, United Kingdom in August 1959. Now 62 years old and semi-retired, he is married with two daughters. Wirral has been his home since he left the Royal Navy in February 1983.*

◆◆◆◆◆

For Britain and Argentina, we servicemen were vital chess pieces in the hands of elected politicians and unelected, military strategists. There's nothing worse than too little strategy, but too much comes in a close second.

And in the Falklands Conflict, strategic overkill sometimes obscured the most vital, human consideration; the mitigation of risk to life and limb. Some might argue that when there's a

1

war on, you should err on the side of defeating your enemy as opposed to preserving your own forces. I tend to disagree.

If you ask HMS Invincible's and HMS Hermes' junior ratings how many enemy aircraft they spotted visually in the South Atlantic, it's likely to be zero. Why? Because our hugely important Queen pieces were largely kept well to the east and heavily shielded throughout. Whilst this plan persevered, lesser vessels and their crews could be tried out here, toyed with there, and sometimes placed into greater jeopardy. 'Risking the few to save the many' is the time-honoured, public rationale. See the attack on HMS Ardent, which can be viewed as a stark reminder of this.

My sympathy goes out to the 52,000 conscripted Argentine servicemen – those still with us – who were pressed into what will have been sold to them as 'service of your country'.

However, this sympathy is tempered when it comes to the unspeakable 38,000 volunteers who had willingly surrendered their civilian status and signed up to serve a murdering, military junta. One that whipped up nationalistic fervour and had the damn gall to masquerade as 'patriotic', even after [4] kidnapping, torturing, and 'disappearing' thousands of its own law-abiding citizens. The Argentine volunteers – a few of whom were navy pilots displaying misplaced bravery – inflicted the greatest casualties to UK forces and would have been fully aware of the junta's murderous actions over the years. How could they not be, following the many well-known protests inside the country?

---

[4] https://adst.org/2014/10/argentinas-dirty-war-and-the-transition-to-democracy/

It beats me how any reasonable, well-adjusted, compassionate human being could risk their own lives, allegedly serve their country, and kill others under the direction of[5] torturing fascists.

A heartfelt message also goes out to all the forgotten UK veterans struggling with the ubiquitous 'Thanks for your service, you're a real hero' sweet talk. Please tread carefully. If you set out believing and investing in this soft-soap – which usually originates from official or media sources – and go around living your life by it, the blight can worm its way inside and cause damage. After leaving the forces and returning home, you may have your uses – for others. Who you are, where you've been and what you've achieved can be pounced upon and hijacked politically. Your friends and family will be overjoyed to have you back, but you could well be praised to the rafters, patronised, and pressurised from all corners of the media into assuming this newfound hero status, thereby pushing their sales, or viewing figures agenda.

If you're contacted – say by an MP – and you're up for getting involved, you'll only succeed in becoming a handy prop for their own self-promotion. Votes and admiration will flood in for your host, who may bask in the glory, but genuine political representation and furtherance of your interests as a civilian will never arrive. Ultimately, you'll risk being praised to high heaven, before being abandoned, left high and dry, and feeling used and dirty. [6] A similar fate is now lying in wait for dedicated NHS doctors, nurses, managers and ancillary staff. The challenge

---

[5]   https://www.amnesty.org/en/documents/amr13/003/1995/en/

[6]   https://www.theguardian.com/society/2021/nov/03/covid-jabs-to-be-compulsory-for-nhs-staff-in-england-from-april

*veterans must face occurs when we're [7] approached and indulged
by powerful but inferior and degraded collections of humanity
such as [8]governments, the UK Ministry of Defence, [9]media
talking heads, captured newspaper editors and dead from the
neck up celebrities, who all present as personifications of rampant, unchecked opportunism.*

*After being trumpeted far and wide, you'll be crowbarred into
your ill-fitting hero clobber, shown off for a while, then cast to the
four winds when they're through. When the penny finally drops for
you what they've been up to, it'll be too late. I can see your thoughts
now as they crystallise. "So, I stand to be fucked the minute I go to
war, and I stand to be fucked the minute I come back."*

*Low value MoD and central government shithouses will give
their public relations strategies the hard sell, claiming 'we care',
and promising much, but delivering nothing of substance –
which always leads to nowhere. The long-term strategy they rely
on is one of watching from the side-lines as veterans struggle.
They'll smile, pay lip service, [10]sprinkle financial crumbs to selected charities, and [11]sit on their hands where serious money is
needed, making half-hearted gestures affecting 'concern', whilst
impatiently waiting for us to pop off, one by one, before moving*

---

[7]   https://www.msn.com/en-gb/news/newslondon/gurkhas-say-more-will-join-downing-street-hunger-strike-over-pension-disparity/ar-AANcWk5?ocid=uxbndlbing#:~:text=unacceptable.

[8]   https://tapnewswire.com/wp-content/uploads/2015/11/poppy_day_corbyn_blair_4601.jpg

[9]   https://i2-prod.mirror.co.uk/incoming/article13536662.ece/ALTERNATES/s615/0_Good-Morning-Britain.jpg

[10]   https://youtu.be/Ar-KWQYh8tk

[11]   https://news.sky.com/story/hundreds-of-vulnerable-armed-forces-veterans-at-risk-of-losing-crucial-help-through-lost-funding-12422203

onto a fresh batch. At the same time, on the world stage, watch them perform. They'll talk tough before the cameras, conjure up elaborate bogus threats, shake fortunes from the magic money tree, spend freely, [12]fund murdering dictators and pursue aggressive, anti-people, toxic military agendas that serve to plunder far-flung resources whilst filling countless more coffins.

Watching all this play out, the question veterans are forced to ask themselves time and again is 'If I'm a hero, why am I being treated like a piece of shit?'

Driven to contemplate suicide when all hope was lost, how many Falklands veterans survived this and other bloody scenarios, [13]only to perish by their own hand years later? Way too many is the answer. Meanwhile, as each ten-year anniversary passes, accompanied by a welter of gushing media articles, we wrongly assume that veterans must have returned to civilian life, blended back in, are making good progress, and are now out of danger.

Please accept my apologies for linking to [14]this, an extensive MOD report, which spent a large but undisclosed sum, cynically striving to minimise the numbers and impact of Falklands veterans' suicides.

[12] https://declassifieduk.org/bae-systems-sold-weaponry-worth-17-6bn-to-saudis-during-yemen-war/

[13] https://wirralinittogether.blog/2021/09/02/the-times-online-an-article-from-june-2007-by-michael-bilton-originally-published-around-the-time-of-the-25th-anniversary-of-the-british-victory-in-the-falklands-conflict-its-claimed-here-that-m/

[14] https://assets.publishing.service.gov.uk/government/uploads/system/uploads/attachment_data/file/307098/20140428_Falklands_Statistical_Release-1982to2013.pdf

Lots of public money, and 21 pages of bureaucratic blood, sweat and tears were invested in the above report, all focused on standing up to veterans, facing them down and proving a point. What a pity the MoD – ensconced in their well-appointed London offices – have never chosen to apply this level of money or diligence into ensuring their heroes don't end up homeless, forgotten or dead by their own hand. Shame on them.

CHAPTER

The Cenotaph

Politicians routinely dishonour the war dead, desecrating the Cenotaph every Remembrance Sunday before the world's cameras. Sombrely dressed from head to toe, moving slowly and with rehearsed solemnity, they're sporting poppies, are keenly aware of how their image is received, and of the electoral benefits

7

attached to [15]'war washing' as they stamp their faces across it all. Meanwhile, we're lumbered with a dominant, unelected, anonymous UK oligarchy sanctioning and promoting it all, whom we cannot get rid of. Ours is a democracy in name only, where the same old phoneys; puppet politicians, royals, peers, senior civil servants, and media talking heads can poison the air, turn on the tears, sob into their hankies, and feign heartache, knowing it pays them dividends. Whilst bowing 'grief stricken' before the monuments, they've also got half an eye focused on their careers and the promotion of their personal and organisational interests. In so doing, [16]they're defiling the memory of countless forgotten, long dead armed forces members.

The system is carefully designed and will default to accommodating the war guilty when called for. This ensures the complicit are ready at a moment's notice to appear chatty and smiling on lightweight TV and radio programmes. Here, unwary viewers and listeners will be drawn in, side-tracked from any warmongering activities and across onto safer ground, e.g., charity work or opening hospices. To those up to their necks in it, it's a game they're very happy to play, where they can escape any consequences for their repugnant behaviour every single time.

These remembrance gatherings are also an annual, very public reminder of cascading, high-level hypocrisy. It's easy to single the culprits out and label them hypocrites, but it's a charge that won't easily permeate their thick skulls as they strut around

---

[15]   https://www.youtube.com/watch?v=SrNpxcoj4f8

[16]   https://wirralinittogether.blog/2021/09/01/sooner-than-encourage-and-protect-the-very-longstanding-honour-and-reputation-of-gurkha-soldiers-whove-made-the-ultimate-sacrifice-or-put-their-lives-on-the-line-to-serve-the-united-kingdom-the-min/

oblivious, enjoying the limelight. They're just too busy parading their arrogance and counterfeit 'respect for the fallen' to notice.

https://upload.wikimedia.org/wikipedia/commons/thum
b/0/0b/Polling_station_sian_%28London%29_%

Politicians can rely upon cloaking themselves from head to toe in fake glory in return for the general election votes of most of the unaware masses, who will register nothing untoward, and trot along, dutifully queueing up in their millions every five years – as directed by the idiot box in the corner – ready to be relentlessly crapped upon and lied to all over again.

Such rancid activities were deeply shocking to me until I stopped watching TV and buying newspapers a decade ago. It'll be massively insulting now to veterans unfortunate enough to have known and experienced the harsh realities of war, but who haven't yet fought their way out from beneath the comfort blanket of seasoned, high-lustre propaganda.

If we cast our minds back to 1982, does tooling up and travelling most of the way across the globe at huge expense to rescue a forgotten outpost still feel like a noble undertaking? Or is it all feeling rather hollow? Have the long-liberated Falkland Islanders and their sons and daughters suddenly forgotten us? We'll explore this question later.

Also, in 1982, were the islanders' interests, 'paramount', as Thatcher kept claiming, or were somebody else's desires secretly to the forefront?

Few people are aware, but a tiny, vanishing minority of Falkland Islanders owned the land they lived and worked on. Back then, practically 90% of Falklands land, including the vast sheep farms, belonged to the UK-based [17] Coalite Group PLC (40%) and [18] absentee landlords (50%), most of them [19] resident in the UK.

I'd imagine Coalite Chairman Ted Needham and many of these landowners would have been dyed-in-the-wool Thatcher supporters, residing in Tory heartlands, and following the Argentine invasion, were super keen on lobbying for a task force to be raised urgently – whatever the potential pitfalls – in an attempt to recover their stolen property portfolios.

---

[17]   https://wirralinittogether.blog/2021/11/26/31ˢᵗ-march-1982-coalites-request-for-britain-to-maintain-a-naval-presence-in-the-falkland-is-lands/

[18]   https://www.theguardian.com/theobserver/2002/mar/17/features.magazine37#:~:text=After the British,and accom modation.

[19]   https://www.newyorker.com/magazine/2020/07/06/how-prosperi-ty-transformed-the-falklands#:~:text=This was a common pattern%3A the early owners lived on the land%2C but by the twentieth century most farms were held by absentee landlords in Britain%2C or by the Falkland Islands Company—the Falklands equivalent of the East India Company%2C combining trade with governance

https://upload.wikimedia.org/wikipedia/commons/thumb/
c/cf/International_newspapers_at_a_suburban_newsagent

The UK BBC, popular media and newspapers curiously failed to cover these largely hidden interests during the heat of the conflict in 1982 – and still haven't achieved any openness or transparency on this 40 years later.

How could that happen?

"There's no shame in admitting you were bamboozled - all of us are from the earliest age. The dignity comes from knowing better, and resolving to never allow yourself to be fooled in the same way again" –

[20]*Mark Devlin*

---

[20]   http://www.djmarkdevlin.com/

CHAPTER

ABOUT THE BOY

JRO Paul

In February 1976, *I joined naval training school HMS Ganges. I'd been tempted in by [21] Blue Peter's John Noakes and some beguiling TV adverts. The ads offered me the chance to travel the world and build my Royal Navy career. Looking back, I assume all risks to life and limb must have been edited out. Like many more young boys before me, I was extremely willing and eager, but also a naive blank slate queuing up to be scrawled upon.*

+ + ♦ ♦ ♦ + +

---

[21]   https://www.youtube.com/watch?v=sSuZXlUxwbk&

Six years later, I was 22 years old. The average age of those sent to the Falklands was 25. So, I was one of the 'young 'uns' serving onboard [22]HMS Yarmouth (F101).

This was an anti-submarine, Rothesay-class frigate, commissioned in 1960 and based in [23]Rosyth dockyard, near Edinburgh, on the east coast of Scotland. My ship didn't simply hunt submarines. She also doubled up as a stable, floating metal platform which, once dispatched to a great distance, could be used to accurately fling volleys of high explosives onto people whom our politicians had decided needed and deserved them.

In March 1982, my shipmates and I were all in good spirits. We'd completed [24]Exercise Springtrain and had set sail across the Mediterranean to begin our East Asian deployment. Soon we'd be moving south via the Suez Canal and down through the Red Sea, before venturing further east. The sun was up, winds were light, and we were all on a high, primed for our forthcoming travels.

We'd be working hard and spending our days off exploring Naples, Egypt, then further afield. Some time would be spent

---

[22] https://www.youtube.com/watch?v=7L2E3hdcJWc
[23] https://en.wikipedia.org/wiki/Rosyth_Dockyard
[24] https://en.wikipedia.org/wiki/Exercise_Spring_Train

on Gulf Patrol, then it was across to Malaysia and on to many more intriguing places. Having served six years, I was up for this, and keen to travel more broadly with my shipmates before finally calling it a day and leaving the navy. I would then embark on my new working life as a civilian.

But President Leopoldo Fortunato Galtieri Castelli – [25] who later served a brief prison sentence – had been making his own travel plans, which clashed with ours.

So, on 2nd April 1982, the [26] invasion of the Falkland Islands went ahead, Thatcher was tipped off, and [27] an undeclared war was soon to be unleashed on us.

---

[25] http://news.bbc.co.uk/1/hi/world/americas/2650815.stm

[26] https://www.thinkdefence.co.uk/operation-black-buck/invasion-and-force-buildup/

[27] https://historydraft.com/story/falklands-war/article/348#:~:text=the falklands war was a 10-week undeclared war between argentina and the united kingdom

My Falklands War Diary, written on location in 1982

Monday 5ᵗʰ April 1982 (On passage from Gibraltar)

The captain said over the main broadcast that there was a possibility of the ship going to Argentina due to the [28]*Falklands* being invaded and as there were no *RFAs* (Royal Fleet Auxiliary ships) to back us up in the Mediterranean. At 22:15 we were told the ship was turning around and proceeding back to [29]*Gibraltar* at top speed, to arrive by 03:30 to take on ammunition and refuel. On completion of this (2 days maybe) we are to proceed to the South Atlantic with the rest of [30]*the task force*.

[28] https://www.falklands.gov.fk/

[29] https://www.gibraltar.gov.gi/

[30] http://www.naval-history.net/F18-Falklands_War-British_task_force.htm

Looking back, I'm convinced none of HMS Yarmouth's crew had been made aware of [31] the build-up. But soon, news of the Port Stanley assault was out there, and we all got to hear about [32] the fall of the islands' garrison. With this to the forefront of our minds, we left Gibraltar on 5th April 1982, enroute to Naples.

I was working in the MCO that evening, standing over the tele-printer. A FLASH signal came in from Cincfleet (Commander in Chief Fleet), Northwood, UK. I'd been expecting this and watched as the message revealed itself. The orders were clear and unambiguous:

        ... t u r n a r o u n d i m m e d i a t e l y ...
        ... r e t u r n t o G i b r a l t a r ...
        ... r e – a r m, r e – f u e l, t a k e o n s t o r e s ...
        ... j o i n t h e H e r m e s b a t t l e g r o u p ...
        ... p r o c e e d s o u t h ...

This was probably the most momentous radio signal ever received in the long history of F101. Clutching the printout, I raced up to the bridge, in search of the First Lieutenant. Even in the darkness I quickly found him, and he knew what was coming. Peering at it glum-faced he cautioned, "Cardin, don't say a word."

I didn't – but I knew for sure – HMS Yarmouth's 1982 East Asian deployment was now dead and buried.

---

[31] http://news.bbc.co.uk/onthisday/hi/dates/stories/march/19/newsid_2543000/2543639.stm
[32] http://news.bbc.co.uk/onthisday/hi/dates/stories/april/2/newsid_2520000/2520879.stm

[33] *Lord Carrington's resignation letter – Written on 6th April 1982. From a time when a sense of honour still survived among UK cabinet ministers. These days, senior politicians cling to their privileged positions like grim death.* [34] *The relaxed swilling of fine, publicly funded wine is far preferable to giving up office, then having to pay for your damned self.*

Tuesday 6th April (Back in Gibraltar)

The captain cleared the lower deck this morning to tell the ship's company that our Far East deployment was cancelled. We are waiting for [35] *Invincible,* [36] *Hermes* and [37] *Fearless* to arrive in the Gibraltar area, then we will probably accompany them down as far as [38] *Ascension Island.* I heard that it would take two or three weeks for the whole task force to get to the Falklands. This is probably due to the *RFA* vessels being slower. Four civilian merchant ships have been requisitioned by the Ministry of Defence (*Esk, Elk, Tamar,* and *Canberra*). They are now loaded up with marines, SBS, SAS, etc. Argentina has been

---

33 https://www.nytimes.com/1982/04/06/world/carrington-resignation-text.html#:~:text=The Argentine,to me.

34 https://wirralinittogether.files.wordpress.com/2021/12/relax-and-drink-up-chaps.jpg

35 https://www.militaryfactory.com/ships/detail.php?ship_id=HMS-Invincible-R05

36 https://www.dailymail.co.uk/news/article-8804887/Falklands-flagship-HMS-Hermes-reaches-final-destination-turned-scrap-metal.html

37 https://en.wikipedia.org/wiki/HMS_Fearless_(L10)

38 https://www.worldatlas.com/articles/where-is-ascension-island.html

preparing for war, drafting troops to southern Argentina. We stocked with ammunition today and will be storing ship tomorrow.

Wednesday 7th April (Still in Gibraltar)

The Argentines have said they will negotiate over the islands, but they will not pull their troops out. Still not sure when we are sailing, probably tomorrow to join up with *Fearless* and a couple of *RFAs*.

By spring 1982 I'd seen a good chunk of the world. I'd matured a bit and had sprouted some early grey hairs. Into the bargain, I was now a fully trained Leading Radio Operator and a very fast touch-typist. Having travelled widely over the last few years, I felt like I'd seen everything (stupid boy, ha ha), but not enough to convince me to sign up for the full 22 years. Six months before the Falklands was invaded, I'd decided to leave, had lodged my 18 months' notice, and I now had a year left to complete.

Thursday 8th April (Still in Gibraltar)

Britain have issued a statement saying a 200-mile limit has been imposed around the Falklands, and that any enemy warships found within the zone are likely to be fired upon. Press agents are embarked upon *Fearless, Hermes, Invincible* and *RFA*s.

A signal has been received telling us to sail at 16:00 today to join *Fearless*.

---

[39]*Just one question was on the lips of 95% of the crew:* [40]*where's the Falklands? It's become clichéd now, but we really were in the dark on this. Soon, we were surprised to discover it was a very distant, forgotten outpost of the former British Empire. After a string of successful post-war independence claims,* [41]*and as the empire shrank back, UK governments had been trying to quietly offload this place since the 1960s. But could it be pulled off without upsetting the mega-patriotic locals? Awkward.*

·‧♦♦♦‧·

---

[39]   https://hansard.parliament.uk/Commons/1982-12-22/debates/2e-7d635a-2eb7-47e4-a34b-3a606c1d4e0f/FalklandIslands(Shackle-tonReport)#:~:text=some opposition members discovered where the falkland islands were only after april 1982.

[40]   https://www.youtube.com/watch?v=j1XomrBRzwg

[41]   https://www.washingtonpost.com/news/worldviews/wp/2015/09/08/map-the-rise-and-fall-of-the-british-empire/

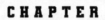

CHAPTER

6

8th April to 9th May

8th April to 9th May

The passage down to the South Atlantic was un-eventful to start with. We sailed at an average speed of 20 knots toward Ascension Island. We arrived there on 16th April. The weather was really hot (close to 100 degrees Fahrenheit). Ascension Island is in the middle of the Atlantic, roughly in line with the River Amazon entrance in South America. We stayed in Ascension for two days and I got some good fishing in. We left there on 18th April. We slowed down a bit on orders from the Ministry of Defence as negotiations took place between Britain and Argentina with the US Secretary of State acting as a go-between. Haig peace bid failed, and hostilities flared up. The Argentine cruiser *General Belgrano* was torpedoed by the British submarine *HMS Conqueror*. 300+ lives were lost out of the 1,000 Argentinian crew members.

Within the above diary notation is a glaring piece of misinformation, likely to have originated on the BBC World Service. I made the mistake of unwittingly jotting it down at the time, assuming it to be legit. The statement "Haig peace bid failed, and hostilities flared up" is wide of the mark. The Haig peace bid didn't 'fail', and hostilities didn't 'flare up' as if from nowhere. The peace bid was in fact 'torpedoed' by the UK government, who were eager to follow this up immediately with genuine, armed Mark 8 torpedoes.

2nd May 1982 – [42]'No going back'. [43]The sinking of the Argentine cruiser ARA General Belgrano at 18:57 BST outside the Total Exclusion Zone (TEZ) – whilst sailing away from the islands – and with an eventual loss of 368 lives, created much concern in the task force, and within the UK Parliament.

There was no going back after this. Out-and-out war became a foregone conclusion. We all knew it in our heart of hearts, but few of us breathed a word.

Peruvian President [44]Fernando Belaunde Terry's proposed peace plan had been presented to Thatcher's Peruvian Ambassador Charles Wallace in Lima [45]at midday on Saturday 1st May, the day before the sinking. Its receipt would have been officially

---

[42]   http://belgranoinquiry.com/timelines#:~:text=Sunday 2 May,of the Belgrano.
[43]   https://hansard.parliament.uk/Commons/1982-05-04/debates/669c9a35-04f7-4ece-b7a7-d63fac70286b/Engagements
[44]   https://www.upi.com/Archives/1982/05/02/Perus-President-Fernando-Belaunde-Terry-said-Sunday-that-Britain/4525389160000/
[45]   http://belgranoinquiry.com/article-archive/the-peruvian-peace-plan#:~:text=Arias Stella also,the British Government.st May

acknowledged. Thatcher later [46] lied straight-faced on BBC TV whilst on the election trail in May 1983, quoting 'our boys' to curry votes, and suggesting that the peace proposals "did not reach London until after the attack" on Sunday 2ⁿᵈ May.

As was customary, the UK's man in Lima, [47] Ambassador Charles Wallace, would have followed up immediately around midday on Saturday 1ˢᵗ May with a FLASH telegram from Lima to London, describing the seven points of the peace plan – in detail, not in outline. I've searched for this crucial document in the UK National Archives but can't locate it.

As a professional communicator I knew that 40 years ago the telegram was a well used method and one of the most rapid and reliable means of transmitting textual information accurately over long distances. There was a strict protocol here as regards the timestamped recording of transmission and acknowledgment of receipt. The records verifying this will exist somewhere and the records don't lie. [48] Some of those who were in receipt of this information didn't lie either.

Only a deeply dishonest individual would argue they hadn't received any word from mediator Al Haig or their own ambassador AND hadn't received [49] a follow-up telegram 14 hours after

---

[46]   https://youtu.be/3JZlP5qQVtE

[47]   http://announcements.telegraph.co.uk/deaths/176443/wallace

[48]   http://belgranoinquiry.com/article-archive/the-peruvi-an-peace-plan#:~:text=Did Britain know,the Sunday morning.

[49]   http://belgranoinquiry.com/timelines#:~:text=british ambassador wallace relays info to uk (

it had been sent. [50] Or worse, that an 'outline' version of events took 17 hours to reach them, during which time they'd gone ahead, issued an order to torpedo a ship, and killed 368 sailors.

There is evidence here [51] from the lips of Thatcher herself that in 1982, telegrams were sent and received almost instantaneously.

So, what happened to the [52] Charles Wallace Telegram?

The cover story Thatcher used on BBC TV, describing her version of events as 'fact', whilst hawking for votes, was as insulting as [53] she herself was beneath contempt.

Many prior and subsequent Lima / Wallace telegrams – [54] listed on the Margaret Thatcher website – had been received and acted upon immediately. This time, the stakes could not have been higher. Why did such a reliable process, used in wartime by governments, appear to stumble and go so tragically wrong this time around?

---

50 http://belgranoinquiry.com/article-archive/diana-v-maggie#:~:text=This makes a,and the timezones)

51 https://hansard.parliament.uk/Commons/1982-04-03/debates/43f4bd64-426b-488d-a12e-ade282341db0/CommonsChamber#:~:text=yesterday morning at 8.33 am we sent a telegram which was acknowledged. at 8.45 am all communications ceased

52 https://wirralinittogether.blog/2021/11/22/what-happened-to-uk-ambassador-to-peru-charles-wallaces-telegram-sent-to-london-on-1st-may-1982/

53 http://belgranoinquiry.com/timelines#:~:text=

54 https://www.margaretthatcher.org/search?w=lima+telegram&searchtype=and&t=0&starty=&startm=&startd=&endy=&endm=&endd=&onedayy=&onedaym=&onedayd=

Thatcher's approval rating had been [55] at an extremely low ebb prior to the conflict. Unemployment was high, the country had been through a recession and there was huge dissent within the rank and file of her party.

With hindsight, we can conclude that Thatcher's driving motivation here was not to opt for peace and thereby protect us and preserve the lives of hundreds of Argentine sailors, but to act out of callous, political self-interest, prevent her party splitting down the middle, [56] her government falling from power, and to hell with the consequences.

It wasn't simply a case of a vital, missing telegram. To quote Thatcher from her BBC TV "Nationwide" meeting with Diana Gould: [57] "One day, all of the facts – in about 30 years' time – will be published".

We beg to differ. The MargaretThatcher.org website may have successfully reproduced some of the information, but the Cabinet Office fortress drawbridge has since been raised aloft – possibly for the next 40 years – and we may never get at the critical, concealed information, [58] i.e., the telegram sent by now deceased UK Ambassador Charles Wallace on 1st May 1982:

---

[55]   https://www.upi.com/Archives/1981/12/18/Mrs-Thatcher-called-Britains-most-unpopular-leader-since-WW-II/7728377499600/

[56]   http://belgranoinquiry.com/article-archive/the-peruvian-peace-plan#:~:text=James Prior in,Rogers%2C p.111)

[57]   https://youtu.be/3JZlP5qQVtE?t=224

[58]   https://www.lrb.co.uk/the-paper/v06/n06/tam-dalyell/tam-dalyell-on-the-sunday-sinking-of-the-belgrano#:~:text=On 21 October,British Prime Minister.

Catalogue description

Falkland Islands: political; copies of incoming telegrams

Reference:	CAB 163/374
Description:	Falkland Islands: political; copies of incoming telegrams
Date:	1982 Apr 02 - 1982 Aug 15
Held by:	Creating government department or its successor, not available at The National Archives
Former reference in its original department:	J 150 PART 2 ANNEX
Legal status:	Public Record(s)
Closure status:	Closed Or Retained Document; Open Description
Access conditions:	Retained by Department under Section 3.4

This record is closed and retained by Cabinet Office

Visit the department website

Help with your research

How to use this catalogue

Need more context? View the catalogue description for CAB 163

Have you found an error with this catalogue description? Let us know

When I clicked on "Visit the department website", I was greeted by this [59] not very helpful message:

GOV.UK

→ **Coronavirus (COVID-19)** | Guidance and support

Home > Crime, justice and the law > Your rights and the law

How to make a freedom of information (FOI) request

Contents

— Overview

— Organisations you can ask for information

— How to make an FOI request

— If your request is turned down

Overview

You have the right to ask to see recorded information held by public

---

[59]   https://www.opendemocracy.net/en/opendemocracyuk/cabinet-offices-actions-increase-suspicion-about-secretive-foi-unit-mps-told/

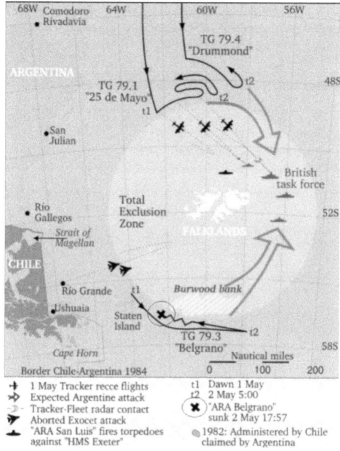

68W Comodoro   64W   60W   56W
     • Rivadavia
                                    TG 79.4
                                   "Drummond"
ARGENTINA
                                              t2   48S
            TG 79.1
           "25 de Mayo"   t2
                t1
      • San
        Julian
                                                    British
                                                    task force
      • Rio   Total
        Gallegos   Exclusion   52S
        Strait of Zone   FALKLANDS
        Magellan
CHILE
        • Rio Grande   t1   Burwood bank
        • Ushuaia
                  Staten
                  Island
                            TG 79.3   t2
      Cape Horn "Belgrano"   Nautical miles   58S
                                0   100   200
Border Chile-Argentina 1984

✈ 1 May Tracker recce flights   t1 Dawn 1 May
⇥ Expected Argentine attack   t2 2 May 5:00
⊃- Tracker-Fleet radar contact   ✖ "ARA Belgrano"
⏴ Aborted Exocet attack   sunk 2 May 17:57
⬥ "ARA San Luis" fires torpedoes   ◌ 1982: Administered by Chile
   against "HMS Exeter"   claimed by Argentina

*https://upload.wikimedia.org/wikipedia/commons/thumb/2/
25/ARA.Belgrano.sunk.svg/640px-ARA.Belgrano.sunk.svg.png*

When and where was the Belgrano sunk?

[60] The Peruvian plan for peace was the launch of a ship, quickly sunk. Pressed souls who were sailing these seas would now sleep, entombed in their bunks.

Truth…who speaks it…? [61] The seven lies.

+ + ♦ ♦ ♦ + +

[60] https://www.independent.co.uk/hei-fi/entertainment/moment-sank-hopes-falklands-peace-deal-7614572.html

[61] http://belgranoinquiry.com/article-archive/seven-lies#:~:text=-Know%2C p.121)-,Major Lies by HMG,the 4th of May.,-The Truth

A couple of days later [62]*HMS Sheffield was hit by an Exocet missile* fired from a Super Etendard fighter. A second missile passed down our starboard side at 1,000 yards as we proceeded to Sheffield's aid. The Arrow also went to help. We tried to put out the fire, but it was too intense. A lot of unspent rocket fuel from the missile ignited. We took six survivors off.

https://upload.wikimedia.org/wikipedia/commons/thumb/e/ef/Hundimiento_del_des
tructor_HMS_Sheffield.jpg/640px-Hundimiento_del_destructor_HMS_Sheffield.jpg

HMS Sheffield hit by Exocet

[62] https://www.youtube.com/watch?v=-uJZkQZG8Zo

[63] *20 were killed approximately, 30 injured.*

While we were giving assistance, torpedoes were fired from a submarine in the area. We came out of that unscathed. The *Sheffield* was abandoned when there was a danger of the *Sea Dart* missile magazine exploding. It didn't go up and she was left to drift. A couple of days later, [64]*we were told to tow her to the east to be picked up by the tug Salvageman*, but the weather worsened, and she started taking in water through the holes in her sides. She went on her side, and we cut the towline.

Before all this, [65]*South Georgia was recaptured.*

The Argentinians claimed that *HMS Exeter* was sunk (she was in Belize at the time of the claim).

https://upload.wikimedia.org/wikipedia/commons/thumb/e/e0/Cap._Augusto_Bedacarratz.jpg/640px-Cap._Augusto_Bedacarratz.jpg

Super Etendard pilot Captain Augusto Bedacarratz

They also claimed that fighting went on for over a week in South Georgia. It was two days. One day for Grytviken and a further day for another settlement on the other side of South Georgia.

[63] https://www.youtube.com/watch?v=IUZu8bvxJs4

[64] https://geriatricgapyears.files.wordpress.com/2017/05/img_0015.jpg

[65] https://www.bbc.co.uk/history/recent/falklands/falklands_gallery_02.shtml

The United Nations, led by Secretary General Pérez de Cuéllar offered to find a solution, originally not wanted by Thatcher but later accepted. Argentinians are insisting on sovereignty. Britain want the Argentinians off the island as called for in the [66]*UN Charter Resolution 502.* Talks are going ahead.

[67]*The Total Exclusion Zone was imposed on 30th April 1982*

On 5th *May 1982 a [FLASH] telegram was sent by* [68]*UK Ambassador Sir Nicholas Henderson in Washington to the Foreign and Commonwealth Office. This followed the concealed snubbing of the Peruvian peace plan, the sinking of ARA Belgrano, and the Exocet strike upon HMS Sheffield. Despite the diplomatic language, there's no mistaking that following the sinking of the Belgrano and the Exocet attack on HMS Sheffield,* [69]*the United States was expressing serious misgivings over the UK's negotiating position.*

---

[66] http://unscr.com/en/resolutions/502

[67] https://military-history.fandom.com/wiki/Total_Exclusion_Zone#:~:text=The Total Exclusion Zone (TEZ) was an area,may have been fired upon without further warning.

[68] https://www.independent.co.uk/news/obituaries/sir-nicholas-henderson-diplomat-who-secured-american-help-for-britain-during-the-falklands-war-1647309.html

[69] https://wirralinittogether.blog/2021/11/10/national-archives-cab129-214-21-peruvian-peace-deal-haigs-misgivings-over-british-position/

Monday 10th May (In Total Exclusion Zone)

We were towing [70] *HMS Sheffield* out of the TEZ, but the weather deteriorated, and she sank this morning. She was still smouldering from the fire which had almost gutted her and peeled all the paint off from the bridge backwards.

We are now proceeding back to the main group. *The Daily Telegraph* say the Argentinians have only four [71] *Exocet* missiles left.

[72] *An Argentine fishing vessel captured by the Royal Navy* was said to be spying (an Argentine naval officer was onboard). Was attacked by helicopters. Later it sank while under tow (*Narwal*).

---

[70]   https://www.theguardian.com/uk/2000/sep/26/falklands.world

[71]   https://www.mbda-systems.com/product/exocet-am-39/

[72]   https://medium.com/@CarlUpshon/sbs-operators-prove-argentinian-trawler-was-a-spy-ship-c15ea8f3177f

CHAPTER

8

The 40ᵗʰ anniversary is no time to celebrate. It's a time to remember the lives lost. The main purpose of this book is to highlight a shrewd political deception, long in the making, passed down, inherited, and played out across many years. This was a simmering hot bed of political intrigue, all carried on behind the backs of the Falkland Islanders and the British and Argentine people.

An unsavoury desire to keep the sensitive details out of public view [73] first came as early as 1969. Unbeknown to us, the secretive double-dealing picked up speed and intensified under Thatcher, [74] while her popularity was tanking. This came to a

---

[73] https://hansard.parliament.uk/Lords/1969-07-10/debates/76e934b2-0e57-4dec-8739-de3889a31742/FalklandIslandsAndTheArgentine?highlight=falkland islands#:~:text=My Lords%2C as,far been confidential.

[74] https://www.theguardian.com/politics/2012/mar/17/margaret-thatcher-papers-tory-split#:~:text=the autumn of 1981 brought margaret thatcher's darkest hour. riots in brixton and toxteth had sent her personal ratings plunging below even those of michael foot%2C and she became the least popular prime minister in polling history.

head in the lead up to the April 2nd, 1982, invasion. Although a few crumbs of information emerged at the time, the full details were suppressed for three decades post-conflict. All the senior players – most of whom had kept everything under their hats – are now dead.

After the British victory, Thatcher turned success in the South Atlantic to her own home-based, political advantage, and the Conservative Party moved swiftly to secure a firm bridgehead for the June 1983 election. [75]Here, they triumphed with almost military efficiency, scoring victories in three main areas:

➢ *An unexpected extension to their political power*
➢ *Renewed geopolitical influence for a once great, but now faltering and receding empire*
➢ *A chance to polish and consolidate their seats at the international top table*

These had been their unstated ambitions all along. They also enjoyed a much longer lifespan on this earth than [76]907 dead soldiers, sailors, airmen and civilians.

This tragic outcome was a direct result of the UK and Argentine governments' prior, reprehensible conduct.

We waited 25 years to see the document below. Here, it's quite staggering to see Foreign Office Minister [77]Nicholas Ridley's pre-conflict activity as he swanned off to the Hotel du Lac in

---

75 https://en.wikipedia.org/wiki/1983_United_Kingdom_general_
 election
76 https://www.liquisearch.com/falklands_war/casualties
77 https://www.theguardian.com/uk/2005/jun/28/falklands.past

Geneva, unseen, and behaved in a manner that clashed directly with Thatcher's subsequent wartime stance. Instead of being upfront about it, Thatcher and Ridley had colluded to secretly push for trade deals, a 99-year leaseback, and the ceding of sovereignty to Argentina, all done behind our backs.

https://upload.wikimedia.org/wikipedia/commons/thumb/4/4b/Vevey_-H%C3%
B4tel_du_Lac.jpg/640px-Vevey_-H%C3%B4tel_du_Lac.jpg

The Hotel du Lac, Geneva, Switzerland

SECRET

[Text of exploratory proposal handed by Mr Ridley in manuscript
to Comodoro Cavandoli on 11 September 1980.]

1.   Titular sovereignty over the Falkland Islands (Islas Malvinas)
and their maritime zone would be transferred to Argentina, with
effect from the date of signature of the Agreement.

2.   Continued British administration of the Islands and their
maritime zone, with a view to guaranteeing to the Islanders and their
descendants the uninterrupted enjoyment of their way of life under
British institutions, laws and practices, would be simultaneously
assured by means of a lease-back to the United Kingdom for a period
of 99 years.   The terms of such a lease would be subject to
periodic review, by agreement between the two parties.

3.   The British and Argentine flags would be flown side by side on
public buildings on the Islands.

4.   The British Government would be represented by a Governor who,
together with a locally-elected Council, would be responsible for the
administration of the Islands and their inhabitants.

5.   The Argentine Government would be represented by a Commissioner-
General.

6.   There would be a Joint Council to arrange co-operation over the
economic development of the Islands and their maritime zone.

SECRET

The secret meeting, also known as Nicholas Ridley's 9/11

[78]*Wikipedia's history of the Falklands sovereignty dispute. The context here is poor, with no mention of Argentina's long involvement in* [79]*President Richard Nixon's and Secretary of State Henry Kissinger's Operation Condor and "Dirty War".*

[80]*Nicholas Ridley's involvement in secret negotiations with Argentina – Fortress Falklands was deemed unfeasible on the grounds of cost.* [81]*The full report, which described this meeting in close detail was released 30 years later. This amounted to conclusive evidence that – pre-conflict –* [82]*the Thatcher government were seeking to rid themselves of this forgotten, distant dot on the map.*

[78]   https://en.wikipedia.org/wiki/Falkland_Islands_sovereignty_dispute
[79]   https://en.wikipedia.org/wiki/Operation_Condor#U.S._involvement
[80]   https://en.wikipedia.org/wiki/Nicholas_Ridley,_Baron_Ridley_of_Liddesdale#:~:text=When,paramount
[81]   https://c59574e9047e61130f13-3f71d0fe2b653c4f00f32175760e96e7.ssl.cf1.rackcdn.com/BAD0573864714A95838DC583BF8C50C0.pdf
[82]   https://penguin-news.com/headlines/politics/2021/an-islanders-memories-of-the-1971-communications-agreement-between-the-falkland-islands-and-argentina/#:~:text=The beleaguered Councillors,in the water.

＋＋＋＋＋＋

1. *The future of warfare:* [83] *Technomancers*
   – Human Augmentation #1. The USA.

2. *The future of warfare:* [84] *The Dawn of a New Paradigm*
   – Human Augmentation #2. The UK.

Note how these speculative, sci-fi style departures from [85] *reality are couched in the weak justification of a "bogeyman" claim; that our enemies (none specified) are likely to be doing the same already (no evidence provided), so we need to be doing it first. Yes, that tired old chestnut.*

＋＋＋＋＋＋

---

[83] https://www.cnbc.com/2021/06/17/anduril-turning-us-troops-into-invincible-technomancers-palmer-luckey-says.html

[84] https://www.gov.uk/government/publications/human-augmentation-the-dawn-of-a-new-paradigm

[85] https://off-guardian.org/2021/10/24/the-banners-of-the-king-of-hell-advance/

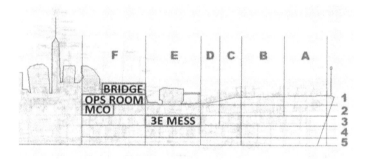

HMS Yarmouth's (incomplete) Deck Plan, as I remember it

To set the domestic scene, I was the Leading Hand of the Mess in charge of 3E deck space, two decks beneath the 4.5-inch gun. This was the living quarters for around 12 sailors, plus a detachment of 12 Royal Marines, desperate to get their hands on their weapons, to feel some firm ground beneath their boots, and to turn their boyhood dreams of neutralising enemy troops into reality. To their dismay, this opportunity never arrived. Try and envisage 24 men – half of them trained to kill, half of them not – crammed together in a space smaller than a tennis court, but with metal bulkheads all around and a lid on top.

Sometimes we couldn't sleep. The hoist that lifted 4.5-inch shells to the gun above us was often clattering away through the night during the NGS [86]*(Naval Gunfire Support) bombardments. We got to know each other well, and things got tense during the low points.* [87]*Disharmony between the RN and RM can be bad at times, even tragic.*

Tuesday 11th May

Talks have been reported to have reached the crucial stage at the UN. Argentina still appears to want sovereignty very soon. Britain are not very optimistic about the talks succeeding.

HMS Alacrity went into Falkland Sound, between the two islands. [88]*She opened fire on an Argentine tanker with 4.5-inch ammunition.* There was a large explosion. She was doing an NGS at the time. There are rumours that the troops will be landed this Sunday.

[89]*Fearless group (amphibious forces)* is now halfway between here and Ascension. Still no mention for *Yarmouth* on BBC World Service. *British Esk* is on her way back today with mail onboard.

---

[86]   https://military.wikia.org/wiki/Naval_gunfire_support

[87]   https://www.dailymail.co.uk/news/article-10070499/Admiral-Sir-Tony-Radakin-accused-undermining-Marines-general-killed-himself.html

[88]   https://en.wikipedia.org/wiki/HMS_Alacrity_(F174)

[89]   https://wikimili.com/en/British_naval_forces_in_the_Falklands_War#:~:text=Beach-,hms fearless,-HMS

Ship that *Alacrity* fired at was reported by Britain to have sunk. Heard on World Service.

Britain and Argentina have both reported substantial progress in the UN talks. The British representative says the next couple of days could be decisive.

Argentina have announced that any British ship approaching the area of operations will be treated as hostile and will be dealt with accordingly.

Wednesday 12ᵗʰ May

The Times reported *HMS Plymouth* was fired at with *Exocet* as she proceeded to the aid of *Sheffield*. This was us really. Plymouth were bronzying in Ascension Island 3,000 miles away!

HMS Plymouth was the first ship I ever served on, aged 17 – for two and a half years – starting in November 1976.

Highlight: A summer 1978 jaunt to Halifax, Nova Scotia, on down the United States east coast; Boston, Bridgeport, Norfolk.

Lowlight: On my first day, I was sent on an errand to the Master at Arms office to ask the burly, angry looking Chief Petty Officer who worked there for a "thick regulator for the showers."

⁕✦✦✦⁕

*Definition: regulator = ship's police officer

17:00 AIR RAID WARNING RED

[90]*HMS Brilliant shot down two out of three Skyhawks* that were attacking the force. A further air raid got through and [91]*hit HMS Glasgow with a bomb which failed to explode* but passed right through the ship (probably 1,000-pound bomb). One casualty suffering from shock. One of the engine intakes damaged beyond immediate repair. *Glasgow Seadart* reset at wrong moment, allowing the air raid access to hit *Glasgow*. We were at action stations for 45 minutes. A friendly helicopter ditched in the sea to the east of us with four crew onboard. All picked up by another helo. A further air raid occurred at approximately 18:30. Sea Harriers were sent up from *Hermes* to intercept two enemy aircraft, unidentified as yet. Air raid warning still red.

I was also the leading hand in charge of the Starboard Watch communications team working in the MCO. This was beneath the Operations Room, which in turn was located within the superstructure. The Ops Room was the ship's nerve centre. I'd been told that [92]Exocet missiles were designed to home in on

[90]   https://www.seaforces.org/marint/Royal-Navy/Frigate/F-90-HMS-Brilliant.htm#:~:text=she was the first royal navy warship to fire the sea wolf missile in action when%2C on 12 may 1982%2C she shot down three a-4 skyhawks

[91]   http://www.naval-history.net/F62-Falklands-British_ships_lost.htm#:~:text=Wednesday 12th,21st May

[92]   https://whitefleet.net/2017/05/28/falklands-war-cruise-missiles/

the most substantial area of the targeted vessel, which made sense as this is often where these nerve centres are located. For us, a direct missile hit on the Ops Room would incapacitate the ship's radar / electronic warfare systems, kill, or severely injure everyone in the vicinity, and be likely to damage the MCO and bridge also. Unlucky us if a missile ever got through. Despite this dark prospect hanging heavy over us, the radio ops on Yarmouth remained an upbeat, happy-go-lucky, and positive bunch.

19:15 AIR RAID WARNING YELLOW

Glasgow incident has been given a press blackout. Nothing heard about it from either Britain or Argentina on the world news. UN talks are said to be progressing by British, but no comment from Argentina. Daily Mail reports a diplomatic sell-out by Thatcher government, giving out a package of concessions to Argentina. Media fears that the three remaining Argentinian submarines will concentrate on the amphibious group (*Fearless, Intrepid, RFA Sir* classes, etc.) now that the Argentinians have extended their operations zone to cover the entire South Atlantic. *Fearless* group are now about 700 miles from the Total Exclusion Zone.

About Argentine submarines and the threat they carried; I became aware of a rumour at the time that one or more tactical [93]nuclear depth bombs were being secretly passed between UK ships during the conflict. On 20th May 1982, Labour politician Tam Dalyell MP [94]appeared to refer to this in a vague manner in the UK Parliament. If true, I think highly sensitive information such as this being leaked and made public would have created uproar. In the UK, the general perception of nuclear weapons was then and is now that they are non-tactical and a final option, only to be used as part of a MAD or Mutually Assured Destruction scenario. I could never know for sure whether the UK task force was carrying

---

[93] https://www.opendemocracy.net/en/britains-other-nuclear-weapons/#:~:text=All the navy,was nuclear-capable

[94] https://hansard.parliament.uk/Commons/1982-05-20/debates/e348886e-0a6a-486a-b54d-dcc1c6b1122f/FalklandIslands?highlight=tam nuclear#:~:text=Incidentally%2C on the subject of nuclear weapons%2C may I ask one question%3A are we infringing the treaty of Platelco%2C which establishes Latin America as a nuclear-free zone%3F

concealed [95] *tactical nuclear depth bombs / mortars, but Britain did possess them and with the* [96] *benefit of hindsight, judged against what I'd heard at the time, this rumour now appears to have been highly plausible.*

During this conflict, did the United Kingdom breach the 1967 [97] *Tlatelolco Treaty which embargoed all deployment and use of nuclear weapons within that zone?* [98] *It seems possible, but this article denies it.*

If I was to suggest "In late April 1982, HMS Yarmouth took temporary possession of a tactical nuclear bomb and later transferred custodianship to HMS Sheffield" it would possibly land me in hot water. I'm not suggesting that this occurred for one moment.

What I will state is that there were vague references to "THE 1,000lb bomb". My suspicions were alerted by the curious use of the definite article.

Through my communications role, I was relatively 'in the know' and from memory, "THE 1,000lb bomb" was being transferred from ship to ship on a regular basis. I pondered at the time; why

---

[95] http://belgranoinquiry.com/sound-archive/ken-coates-use-of-nuclear-weapons

[96] http://belgranoinquiry.com/article-archive/the-peruvian-peace-plan#:~:text=your task force we knew was bringing nuclear weapons which was an infringement of protocol one of the treaty of tlatalolco which you yourselves had signed

[97] https://www.nti.org/learn/treaties-and-regimes/treaty-prohibition-nuclear-weapons-latin-america-and-caribbean-lanwfz-tlatelolco-treaty/#:~:text=Obligations-,The treaty aims to,in any other way,-The

[98] https://www.nti.org/gsn/article/british-warships-carried-nuclear-weapons-during-falkland-islands-war/

the reliance upon playground level cloak and dagger? I didn't know. Why the inability to refer to this bomb in more definite terms, the way we did with all other armaments? I didn't know.

Post-conflict, it got me thinking, what if it had been a nuclear weapon?

What if one of the ships that was sunk had been carrying "THE 1,000lb bomb"?

What if one or more nuclear bombs are still lying there – [99]like Broken Arrows – 40 years later and have been increasingly left subject to the whims of natural entropy?

EXPOSED. From 3rd January 2022 – [100]exclusive from Declassified UK.

———— ·•◆◆•· ————

British may withdraw from World Cup due to be held this June. Argentina are the holders.

[101]*Pope's visit planned for early June* may be cancelled as he cannot be seen visiting countries that are at war.

Prisoners taken in South Georgia are being repatriated via Ascension / Paraguay.

---

[99] https://www.arcgis.com/apps/Cascade/index.html?appid=96097370c-de9486a918725bbd2257fabs

[100] https://declassifieduk.org/uk-deployed-31-nuclear-weapons-during-falklands-war/

[101] http://news.bbc.co.uk/onthisday/hi/dates/stories/may/29/newsid_4171000/4171657.stm

Thursday 13th May

A quiet day. No incidents reported. Mail should have arrived onboard but was held up by adverse weather, visibility being down to 200 yards. Should be onboard tomorrow. *Hermes, Glamorgan* detached for unspecified operations inshore but later cancelled. On the political front, no definite solution has been reached but the talks are said to be progressing but nearing the crucial stage.

Britain has reported minor damage to *HMS Glasgow* with no casualties.

Galtieri has said Argentine troops are both spiritually and militarily ready for Britain's attack on the Falkland Islands.

Friday 14th May

The weather has improved now.

16:00 Mail has arrived onboard.

UN Secretary General has said the next two days will be decisive. He wants final answers from each country within the next 36 hours. Pym said there was no change in the situation.

Sea Harriers have made more bombing attacks on Port Stanley Airport.

> **Saturday 15th May**
>
> This morning, special forces, inserted on Pebble Island [102] *destroyed six Pucara, one Skyvan and three other unidentified A/C.* Two minor British casualties. One Argentinian casualty. *Glamorgan* backed them up with an NGS.
>
> Talks still going on. Both sides not optimistic.

Pebble Island was purchased for £400 in 1869. [103] *It recently came onto the market again. The sale of* [104] *Carcass Island.*

⋅ ◆ ◆ ◆ ⋅

> **Sunday 16th May**
>
> Galtieri has said he will lose 40,000 troops on the Falklands and will fight, if necessary, for six years.
>
> Argentine supply vessel attacked with Sea Harriers. All bombs missed but vessel was abandoned, and crew were seen in life-rafts. The Junta claimed that the life-rafts were machine gunned from a British warship.
>
> We are taking on mortars tonight.
>
> Port Stanley airstrip bombed again.

[102] https://www.youtube.com/watch?v=tuSXwOKsjdA

[103] https://www.privateislandsonline.com/south-america/falklands/pebble-island

[104] https://www.dailymail.co.uk/travel/travel_news/article-5340903/Meet-man-bought-Falkland-island-30k.html

Monday 17ᵗʰ May

Talks continuing. Nott has said British casualties are to be expected in the ensuing landing on the Falklands. Press are forecasting a British landing very soon.

European Economic Community (EEC) have put off decision about a further month's sanctions against Argentina. Denmark, Italy, and Eire are expressing reservations.

[105] *Talks in New York now at crucial stage* and decision should be made very soon. Argentina have drawn up their statement and decisions following talks. Final phase has now got underway. Thatcher has said this is the last chance for peace.

Tuesday 18ᵗʰ May

Speculation in press and on radio about imminent landing of British forces. Still awaiting Argentine detailed replies.

Wednesday 19ᵗʰ May

Thatcher seems to have turned down final Argentine proposals. War now seems imminent unless Pérez de Cuéllar can come up with something.

---

[105] https://www.jstor.org/stable/20692458?addFooter=false&seq=1

Sea King HC4 of No.846 NAS – embarked on HMS Hermes – crashed into the sea northeast of the islands, believed due to a bird strike, although this is now open to doubt. Of 30 men onboard, 18 men of the SAS, the aircrewman, a member of the Royal Signals and an RAF man were all lost. [106] The two pilots survived.

Thursday 20ᵗʰ May

Landing should be in the early hours of to-morrow morning. UN Secretary General has forwarded final proposals to both countries. Thatcher has called emergency meeting of inner cabinet. Costa Méndez, an Argentine diplomat, has said the only obstacle to peace is the British Prime Minister's intransigence.

We will be at action stations from 01:00 tomorrow morning, probably.

Newspapers received onboard are about 50 per cent fact, 25 per cent educated guesses and 25 per cent fabrication.

Two Harriers bombed Argentine key positions on the Falklands last night. Both returned safely to *Hermes*.

17:00 Thatcher has turned down the final Argentine proposals. Perez de Cuellar's last minute proposals also seem to have been discarded. There is a reported softening in the Argentine

---

[106]   https://www.naval-history.net/F63-Falklands-British_aircraft_lost. htm#:~:text=Wednesday 19ᵗʰ,were saved.

stance over the islands when they asked the United States for a contribution that may lead to a solution The main aim of the landing tomorrow is to secure a bridgehead and set up *Rapier* missile positions. Amphibious landings will take place, also helicopters will ferry troops across. We'll be the first ship to enter the sound followed by *Fearless* and *Intrepid*. We are also down to do an NGS some time.

21:00 We're not the first ship in now, *HMS Ardent* is.

A former Ardent crew member has alleged that the ship may have been used as a distraction from the landings.

[107] *"We were put in the middle of the Sound to draw the enemy aircraft to us … they landed all the troops in San Carlos without casualty. Unfortunately, it was at the cost of HMS Ardent."*

———— ·•♦♦♦•· ————

12:38 AIR RAID WARNING RED

Friday 21ˢᵗ May – The landing is taking place in San Carlos Bay

Antrim and *Argonaut* have been damaged by bombs. *Antrim* has one UXB onboard. *Argonaut*

107   https://www.chroniclelive.co.uk/news/north-east-news/life-changed-ever-falklands-war-1496444

has two UXB onboard. She has no propulsion at the moment. *Broadsword* and *Brilliant* have each shot down an enemy Skyhawk with *Seawolf* missiles.

13:55 Ardent has been hit badly. We are proceeding to render assistance. Too late for firefighting. They are abandoning ship. I was sent up top to help out. The back of the ship is ripped open like a tin can with flames and black smoke pouring out. All the blokes are on the superstructure dressed in survival suits and lifejackets. [108]*Two blokes are stuck behind the fire,* right on the back end. Jumped into sea, both got lifejackets on but no suits. A Wessex helicopter is picking them up. [109]*Alongside the ship now. 168 survivors. 20 missing, 30 injured, some seriously.* Bloke came on with his fingers missing off left hand, bandaged up roughly.

[110]*The injured man may have been this guy, but I'm not sure*

† † ◆ ◆ † †

[108] https://www.maritimeprints.com/portfolio/view/hms-ardent-airlift-rescue-falklands-war/

[109] https://wirralinittogether.files.wordpress.com/2021/05/hms-yarmouth-takes-on-survivors-from-hms-ardent-falklands-conflict.jpg?w=1024

[110] https://youtu.be/T9S0BLMmRnY?t=203

Other bloke's head covered in blood. Most of them suffering shock. It's hard getting them to walk the right way. They're all going down the stokers' and seamen's messes.

They will be transferred to [111]*SS Canberra*. One of the blokes who was winched out of the sea later died, probably from the cold. All the after repair party were killed and probably all the flight crew. The captain is with the survivors.

Three killed on *Argonaut*. Waves of Mirage and Skyhawks coming over, dropping retard bombs. We're answering with 4.5-inch shells and *Seacat* plus small arms fire. We have put a couple off that were intent on hitting us.

Reports coming in of Pucaras and helicopters being shot down. The news tonight reported 17 enemy A/C shot down including four helicopters. A signal report came in saying 17 Mirage / Skyhawks shot down. Two Pucaras and some helicopters.

Argentina claim they lost one aircraft.

---

[111] https://beyondships.com/PO-Canberra-Falklands.html

Saturday 22nd May

11:00 Quiet, no air attacks coming in. Fast patrol boat picked up, coming in to attack. Intercepted by Sea Harrier, beached and on fire.

Quiet again.

16:10 Wave of six Skyhawks coming in. All retreated when intercepted by Harriers.

16:30 Submarine reported by troops on the island. *Plymouth* has gone to have a look. Nothing found.

Except for "Secret" and above, we saw the plain text of all sensitive confidential and restricted messages exchanged between ships, local commanders, and Cincfleet in Northwood. All comms – whether sent via encrypted text, voice, morse code, semaphore or Aldis lamp – were handled through our communications department.

[112] The KL7 encryption / decryption machine – a relic from the 1950s – was used by officers to encrypt / decrypt top secret messages. If anyone knew what was brewing, or what missions HMS Yarmouth would be involved in, it was us. We'd often be stopped in the passageways by men wanting to know what the latest "buzzes" were. A few of us spilled the beans. Others lied. Some of us put our forefinger to our nose and went, "Loose lips sink ships, kid."

We also oversaw the long distance, HF (High Frequency) comms gear and circuits, sending and receiving telegrams or setting up

---

[112]   https://cryptomuseum.com/crypto/usa/kl7/index.htm

remote phone calls between the crew and their families in the UK. This privilege was withdrawn for a couple of months during the heat of battle, but it kicked in thick and fast after the Argentine surrender. So, it was always a good idea to play it cool and keep us fellas sweet. We could be very useful.

I'd say I'd earned my Communications Branch privileges after spending 22 weeks – including the long hot summer of 1976 – sweating like a pig in a classroom that doubled as a sauna, learning to touch-type, process messages and to send and receive Morse code at the [113] now vanished HMS Mercury training base in Petersfield, Hampshire. Back then, this was by far the longest basic training for any Royal Navy branch.

Sunday 23rd May

03:00 Patrolling Falkland Sound. Picked up radar contact. Found to be [114] *MV Monsunen* (Falklands cargo vessel, taken over by the Argentinians). *HMS Brilliant*'s Lynx helo has gone to have a look and was fired at. He is being told on [115] *Channel 16* to switch on his navigation lights and to stop, but he's ignoring us.

We're firing star shells to suss him out. He's dodging in and out of coves and is difficult to find on radar.

---

[113]   https://www.youtube.com/watch?v=NO5Zx-cKVwk

[114]   https://www.iwm.org.uk/collections/item/object/205189460

[115]   http://www.csgnetwork.com/marinefreqtable.html#:~:text=EPIRBs-,16,watch on this channel,-17

05:15 Firing live ammunition at it. He has ignored repeated warnings to stop and switch on lights. Suspect he has been hit.

Arrived back at San Carlos Bay safely. *Ambuscade* Lynx hit an FPB (Fast Patrol Boat) – neutralised. Two Puma helos hit by Sea Harriers.

16:30 AIR RAID WARNING RED

Mirages and Skyhawks coming in. [116]*Broadsword's Seawolf splashed a Skyhawk that was attacking Antelope.* Wreckage crashed into *Antelope*'s main mast. First reports say one dead, two injured. They keep coming in for further attacks. Five Mirage shot down, one Skyhawk shot down, and one possible Mirage, two possible Skyhawks. No losses on our side reported as yet.

20:55 Getting dark now. Don't foresee any more air raids tonight.

---

[116] http://www.hmsbroadsword.co.uk/falklands/thewar/bomb_alley_day_1.htm#:~:text=Fortunately Leading, port wing *Seawolf* splashed a Skyhawk that was attacking Antelope

21:05 HANDS FALL OUT OF ACTION STATIONS

We're RASing [117](*Replenishment at Sea*) tonight as we are down to only 20 per cent fuel remaining. *Broadsword* RASing also. We should be back in San Carlos before daylight.

https://upload.wikimedia.org/wikipedia/commons/thumb/5/5b/Explosi%C3%B3n_de_la_bomba_en_la_fragata_HMS_Antelope.jpg/

HMS Antelope UXBs explode

[118]*The wreckage that hit Antelope dropped two UXB on her.* After leaving harbour tonight there were loud explosions reported from her direction. Later on an even louder explosion. Probably *Exocet* magazine.

117 https://www.globalsecurity.org/military/world/europe/rfa-ras-in-tro.htm

118 https://www.youtube.com/watch?v=7B5zlPB-yrU

Monday 24ᵗʰ May

Heard this morning that bombs had exploded on *Antelope*, probably whilst being defused. Heavy casualties reported. We RASd last night. More fuel taken on. We're back in the same position in San Carlos Bay today (Wreck Point).

10:30 AIR RAID WARNING RED

Overflown by Mirage / Skyhawks.

14:20 Being attacked by four Skyhawks (we splashed one with small arms 20mm fire). *Rapier* missiles seen firing as well. *Hermes* CAP (Combat Air Patrol) have shot down three out of four Mirages (the fourth one escaped to the west). All had jettisoned bombs on sight of the two Harriers. *Rapiers* claimed three today.

News reports seven Argentinian A/C shot down today so far. No more raids after these for the rest of the day. Don't know whether any Argentinian A/C got back to the mainland. If none returned, then maybe they'll realise they're losing too many to make it worthwhile attacking us.

12:29 AIR RAID WARNING RED

Tuesday 25th May (Argentina's Armed Forces Day)

Raid forming up in the north.

12:37 One A/C splashed by *HMS Coventry's Sea Dart.*

12:48 AIR RAID WARNING YELLOW

Assessed it was a reconnaissance A/C.

15:30 AIR RAID WARNING RED

Only seconds warning of this one. Our port side 20mm brought one down. A bomb missed us by 100 yards on the port side. Landed between us and *Fearless.*

15:42 AIR RAID WARNING RED

Possible Mirage picked up on radar. Gone down low. [119]*HMS Coventry attacked and has been hit.* Latest signals say she has turned over. Don't

---

[119]   https://youtu.be/hb58eIZzN6I?t=125

know how many were killed yet. Survivors have been picked up by *Broadsword*.

Helos sent by *Fearless* to help. *Broadsword* hit by UXB.

https://upload.wikimedia.org/wikipedia/commons/thumb/5/52/H%C3%
A9lice_SS_Atlantic_Conveyor.jpg/640px-H%C3%A9lice_SS_Atlantic_Conveyor.jpg

Atlantic Conveyor - hit by Exocet

[120]*Merchant vessel Atlantic Conveyor hit by two Exocet missiles in her port quarter* (the accommodation end of the ship). She has been abandoned, is on fire and it is spreading fast. Don't know number of casualties. She had 20 GR3 Harriers onboard that were due to be land-based soon. Don't know if they'd been taken off previous to this attack or what. Two Argentinian Super Etendards came in low, and each released a missile at approximately 23 miles range.

---

[120]   https://www.youtube.com/watch?v=gd1d4zzlKQY

The reference to '20 GR3 Harriers onboard' was false, possibly caused by the fog of war. On checking Wikipedia, there were 8 Fleet Air Arm Sea Harriers and 6 RAF Harrier GR3 jump jets, but all of these had been off-loaded in mid-May.

The sinking of the Atlantic Conveyor brings to mind an old Scottish oppo of mine – [121]Jock M – who left HMS Yarmouth some time before the conflict broke out. He'd spent forever telling us how pissed off he was with the navy, how he wanted out and how he'd slammed his notice in ages ago. Civvy Street was beckoning, and he was proud to answer that call.

When he left us, we didn't see him for dust. He'd joined another ship and then in April '82 turned up at [122]HMS Nelson, the main shore base in Portsmouth. Here he would spend a week doing his leaving routine, throwing his kit back, and getting his exit chit stamped by each department before saying his goodbyes. But he never got the chance. He was intercepted, and his escape route blocked by some anonymous, high-up busybody. He was kept in, and for good measure, drafted to the [123]Atlantic Conveyor before it set sail for the South Atlantic.

See above for the events of 25th May 1982. [124]Unlike 12 of his crew mates, Jock survived the Exocet attack, abandoned ship, plunged into the deep, unholy chill of the South Atlantic, and had

---

[121] https://www.thinkdefence.co.uk/the-atlantic-conveyor/#:~:text=Colin Muirhead,from Atlantic Conveyer

[122] https://en.wikipedia.org/wiki/HMNB_Portsmouth

[123] https://www.thinkdefence.co.uk/the-atlantic-conveyor/

[124] https://www.atlantic-conveyor.co.uk/action-of-25th-may/heroes

just minutes to find a life raft, clamber onto it and live.[125] As we finally sailed into Rosyth in July, the first happy face we recognised in the massive, welcoming crowd was [126]Jock M, jumping about in a frenzy, and frantically waving his arms at us.

I haven't met him since, but I hope to catch up with him again one day. I hope you're reading this, Jock…

⋅⋅◆◆◆⋅⋅

On the political side, [127]*the British Government won't accept the ceasefire put forward by Ireland.* The UN Security Council has adjourned its emergency meeting. Nott says Argentina have lost more than 50 fixed wing A/C and cannot go on with such losses.

Coventry incident has been reported on the World Service News (ship's name not mentioned yet).

Two merchant supply ships were damaged and have UXBs onboard. No mention yet of the *Atlantic Conveyor* incident on the news.

Britain say three Argentinian A/C shot down today. Argentina say two British Harriers splashed over Port Stanley and Two Sea Kings over Port Darwin.

[125] https://wirralinittogether.files.wordpress.com/2021/05/hms-yarmouth-returns-to-rosyth-july-1982.jpg?w=510

[126] https://www.youtube.com/watch?v=_NGtULfzx5s

[127] https://www.thejournal.ie/anglo-irish-relations-falklands-war-belgrano-723142-Dec2012/

Pilot from A/C shot down by us ejected into bay and was picked up and is being held on the *Fearless*. Press blackout in force on the two ships hit until tomorrow.

Wednesday 26th May

Atlantic Conveyor and *Coventry* both mentioned on this morning's news. Harrier A/C were safely taken off before the *Exocet* attack, but millions of pounds' worth of equipment lost and still no mention of casualty numbers.

Couple of air raid reds during afternoon but both spurious.

Off-loading of equipment and stores goes on in the bay, using landing craft and helos.

16:10 Heads up west.

16:53 AIR RAID WARNING RED

Possible attacks from both east and west.

17:15 No further indication of attack. Two came in and jettisoned bombs south of us. Explosions on the hills.

18:00 News reports four dead on *Atlantic Conveyor*. 20 dead and 20 injured on *Coventry*.

Speculation that last air raid was a decoy to allow them to return their Super Etendards to the mainland.

Learnt that *Atlantic Conveyor* was hit by only one *Exocet*. The other missed, apparently.

Thursday 27th May

Nine were killed on *Atlantic Conveyor* (mostly civilians).

14:30 AIR RAID WARNING RED

Coming in low over the land. Sea Harriers intercepting.

Latest news says 12 men were killed on *Atlantic Conveyor* including the captain, who was last seen getting in a life-raft, which drifted towards the ship.

Advance has begun from the bridgehead, Thatcher stated in House of Commons today. Met with cheers from the Tory side of the house. News reports that Argentinian agents are scouring the world for a willing supplier of the French-built *Exocets* which have proved so effective. Price of the missile has been said to have increased from $200,000 to $1,000,000 per missile.

5,000 British troops are reported advancing.

15:26 HMS Argonaut on fire. No info in yet. Not the result of an air raid though.

16:10 AIR RAID WARNING RED – from the west.

16:20 AIR RAID WARNING YELLOW

Argonaut fire may be the result of a welding accident. A lot of steam seen coming out (maybe steam drenching?)

18:00 Argonaut fire was a welding accident, easily controlled.

News: [128]*United States have reported they are providing Britain with Sidewinder missiles plus other arms.*

[129]*Leopoldo Galtieri was among the* [130]*United States' closest allies in the 'Dirty War', a brutal programme that kidnapped and*

---

[128]   https://www.standard.co.uk/news/world/cia-files-reveal-how-us-helped-britain-retake-the-falklands-7618420.html

[129]   https://www.youtube.com/watch?v=2BX55_Ddp-k

[130]   https://en.wikipedia.org/wiki/Operation_Condor#:~:text=the united states government provided planning%2C coordinating%2C training on torture%2C%5B19%5D and technical support and supplied military aid to the juntas during the johnson%2C nixon%2C ford%2C carter%2C and the reagan administrations.%5B2%5D such support was frequently routed through the cia.

murdered law-abiding South Americans. Mindful of his loyalty to this, towards the end of the conflict, Ronald Reagan withdrew somewhat, selfishly segueing across to his own extra-judiciary 'backyard' interests, and [131]pleading with Britain not to retake the islands by force.

Tonight, we shot down one Skyhawk, and another went over the hills leaking fuel (wouldn't have made it back). One of our *Seacats* made a pilot eject. He was picked up in a boat by marines.

British war graves at Ajax Bay

Rapiers on land claimed two, possibly three out of four Skyhawks who were bombing shoreside positions. Hospital buildings have three UXB. Came in through the roof over in Ajax Bay. Four marines killed, 20 injured (some bombs must have exploded).

---

[131]   https://www.nytimes.com/2012/12/29/world/europe/falklands-war-caused-rare-friction-for-thatcher-and-reagan.html

Friday 28ᵗʰ May

We did an early morning NGS today at Port Howard. Was successful. *Arrow* did one on Port Darwin. We're doing one on Port Darwin tonight.

Port Howard

Port Howard is the largest settlement on West Falkland. It is in the east of the island, on an inlet of Falkland Sound. It is on the lower slopes of Mount Maria.

W Wikipedia

Population: 22 (2012)

Weather: 8°C (46°F), Rain showers   See more

Quiet day so far. No air raids.

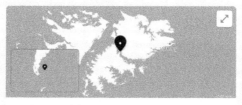

Darwin, Falkland Islands
Falkland Islands

Darwin is a settlement in Lafonia on East Falkland, Falkland Islands, lying on Choiseul Sound, on the east side of the island's central isthmus, 2.5 miles north of Goose Green. It was known occasionally as Port Darwin.

W Wikipedia

Settled: 1859

Port Darwin NGS cancelled as [132]*paras have captured Darwin and Goose Green* (reported on world news – that's how we first found out).

Argentines have claimed they have launched a counterattack and recaptured all lost ground. This is more propaganda. Three Harriers were sent in to bomb Darwin to help the final blow by the British troops. There were casualties on both sides, mainly Argentines. No definite numbers in yet but maybe over 80 Argentines dead and many injured / taken prisoner. The paras suffered a lot of casualties on their way there, mainly due to attacks by Pucara ground-attack A/C. [133]*Commanding Officer dead (Lt Col. H. Jones).*

---

[132] http://www.naval-history.net/F48goosegreen.htm

[133] https://historylearning.com/modern-world-history/falklands-war-1982/h-jones/

I was around the same age as HMS Yarmouth, the first Rothesay-class frigate ever brought into service. She was the final ship on which I served, and her remains make up several rusted pieces laid out on the North Atlantic Ocean floor. In June 1987, although she was still floating, the time had come for this tired, obsolete vessel to meet her end.

MoD officials are a pragmatic bunch when frittering away public money, and are keen to promote their young, seaborne killing machines as desirable vixens to be swooned over. But they're equally keen – when these seductive damsels' active days are through – to put them to the sword in a cool, calculated manner. So, HMS Yarmouth became target practice for the missiles of HMS Manchester.

This was the fate of several Rothesay-class frigates whose time had come. [134]Before the axe finally fell, another Falklands veteran, sister ship HMS Plymouth – my very first sea posting – was

---

[134] https://www.youtube.com/watch?v=n7a_-9VqyjI

the main attraction of the Birkenhead Warship Preservation Trust, just a mile away from my house.

And not long after HMS Yarmouth's fiery end, HMS Manchester gave up the ghost and was decommissioned in 2011. Which makes me feel pretty over the hill…

Saturday 29ᵗʰ May

Very quiet. One air raid so far (two contacts). One shot down by shoreside *Rapier*. Other one evaded. The pilot managed to eject from the damaged A/C.

[135]*MV British Wye was attacked by an Argentinian C130 Hercules today.* She was miles away from the TEZ on her way to Ascension Island. The Hercules dropped bombs, but all missed. No casualties or damage reported. 1,300 POWs taken at Darwin and Goose Green today. Whole area is now under control of British troops. Before the surrender, the Argentines managed to move a number of aircraft from Goose Green landing strip to Port Stanley airfield. 120 civilians now being looked after by paratroopers.

Vulcans may bomb Port Stanley airstrip tomorrow night.

---

[135]   https://c59574e9047e61130f13-3f71d0fe2b653c4f00f32175760e96e7.
ssl.cf1.rackcdn.com/0199C0B9FAE341AF8439C51CDEE1CB51.pdf

Sunday 30th May

Quiet.

16:26 **AIR RAID WARNING RED**

One explosion ashore. May have been a low-level attack as nothing held on radar.

The Falklands War is a prime example of how supposedly unforeseen conflicts can arise between nations, and how they're prepared for and fought, usually against a background of lacklustre international arbitration and diplomatic posturing.

Pre-21st century, short-term engagements like these seemed to begin with a genuine, illegal incursion or a credible, mounting threat before being met by a response. Was this conflict foreseeable and avoidable?

[136] *The first casualty of war has always been the truth. This was the case in 1982. When ARA General Belgrano was sunk – whilst Thatcher was supposed to be hard at work, evaluating a Peruvian peace plan – we on the frontline were 'mushroomed', i.e., kept in the dark and fed on shit. It wasn't until 21 years later that the following 'truth' emerged.*

---

136   https://quotepark.com/quotes/1942458-aeschylus-in-war-truth-is-the-first-casualty/#:~:text=Translations-,In war%2C truth,Aeschylus,-This

According to a newspaper quoting our own secret services – both of whom can and do lie – the Belgrano, despite [137] steaming for 14 hours on a westerly course, away from the task force and towards Argentina, [138] had been instructed to attack RN ships the day before the sinking, targeting an aircraft carrier and thereby jeopardising the success of Operation Corporate. This 'truth', we're told, was later accepted by Argentina's senior military fascists, some of whom happened to be retired, busy writing their books, and were probably in search of ideas and content.

Nobody knows to this day whether these deeply soiled characters received any reward for their helpful contribution in this regard. But when could liars and killers be taken on trust all of a sudden? This is where supposed official secrets always defer to the interests of the keeper. [139] Engaged, tax paying citizens can never quite get at their content to verify any dubious public statements that are made.

The 44-year-old, poorly armed Belgrano and its escorts would never have managed to place themselves within firing range of our distant, well-shielded carriers, and our politicians and admirals – ensconced in Northwood, London – knew that. Approximately 120 dead ARA Belgrano naval conscripts – whose remains are still lying in the rusted hulk to this day – never wanted to be there, that's for sure. And certainly a lot more than we never wanted them there.

---

[137] https://www.jstor.org/stable/44636703?seq=8#metadata_info_tab_contents

[138] https://www.independent.co.uk/news/uk/politics/belgrano-ordered-to-attack-british-ships-on-day-before-sinking-secret-report-reveals-84183.html

[139] https://www.youtube.com/watch?v=3JZlP5qQVtE

Although civilians are still killed in huge numbers, times have changed in other ways. Gazing from this distance all the way back to the Falklands in 1982, where only three civilians were killed, can now bring a sense of wistful nostalgia. And considering the complete and utter carnage that's been carried out – by relentless, calculated design – ever since, it feels like a throwback to a more straightforward, more honest, less manipulative era. But it's still worth repeating, 'truth is the first casualty of war'.

Since 9/11, the corpse of the truth now gets routinely pummelled beyond recognition before being hastily buried out of sight. Elaborate lies occupy the forefront, and so-called 'wars' have morphed into large-scale, David versus Goliath, glorified, theatrical events and quasi-movie productions led by vested interests and big business diehards. Ruthless, corporate mercenaries are granted leeway to act as military proxies and will knock each other out of the way to get at the huge financial and power spoils linked to the systematic plundering of smaller, much weaker nations. [140] See Halliburton, who've been the 21st century's unashamed trailblazers.

Generals are paid to think, not to kill. Privates are paid to kill, not to think, hence… a curious brand of socialism has long been encouraged within the lower or non-commissioned ranks of western armies. This dictates that soldiers will be expected to fight to the death for their comrades, their brothers in arms. No better incentive exists to squeeze from a soldier or marine every drop of devotion to the cause – whatever that happens to be – than to imply 'YOU'RE ALL EQUAL' and to drip-feed

---

[140] https://mavenroundtable.io/theintellectualist/news/reminder-halliburton-made-39-5-billion-from-the-iraq-war

socialist values into key battle orders. Generals and senior ranks know this very well and follow it to the letter. It's not referred to as socialism of course – what a giveaway that would be – so the whole routine is draped in an elaborate subterfuge. If the top brass can cynically fan the flames and get their soldiers wound up enough, courageous, honest men will give their absolute all. Especially if they think they can rescue their injured pal or die for each other rather than for a tatty flag or an even tattier politician or monarch.

The sheer combined might and power of the people will certainly have risen to the forefront of 2 Para's minds – even subconsciously – during the [141]fixed bayonets charges at Goose Green, and later, those of the [142]Scots Guards and Marines at Mount Tumbledown, near the end of the conflict.

The hardest fought victories originate from the bottom up, never from the top down.

Armed forces members often become depressed upon leaving, and it's not simply because their lives have changed. They quickly discover that unlike their old oppos, they can't trust their new civvy street peers, who themselves have been divided, scapegoated, devalued, and encouraged to hate each other for centuries. It's obviously unfair and wrong to hate all civilians. Nevertheless, it's a standard tactic, originating from the MOD's ivory towers, which gets consciously drilled into impressionable UK armed forces junior ranks.

---

[141]   https://www.youtube.com/watch?v=rYCQlyiUJ-g

[142]   https://www.arrse.co.uk/community/threads/battle-of-mount-tum-bledown-13th-june-1982.164347/

Here on the outside, the concept of socialism, togetherness and people looking out for each other is far too menacing to those who've stolen or inherited their land, wealth, and power. Consolidated power structures feel this threat so very keenly, that such ominous movements for the people will never be allowed to build, embed themselves and take hold. Witness the concerted destruction of Labour Party leader and democratic socialist Jeremy Corbyn, all gleefully carried out by anybody possessing the slightest whiff of mindless, hate-filled prejudice.

> *"Believers in government are supporters of slavery" –*
>
> [143]*Mark Passio*

17:11 AIR RAID WARNING YELLOW

17:39 [144]*HMS Avenger attacked with two Exocet missiles.* She said she shot one down with her 4.5-inch gun and the other one missed. The other one was seduced away by chaff. Skyhawks followed in, dropping bombs, but they missed. Apparently one Skyhawk crashed after dropping six bombs. Avenger picking up wreckage.

---

[143]   http://www.whatonearthishappening.com/-

[144]   https://www.independent.co.uk/news/obituaries/admiral-sir-hugo-white-commander-who-fought-exocet-attacks-during-falklands-war-and-was-later-governor-gibraltar-9588010.html

Monday 31st May

After *Avenger* incident, Argentinians claimed that two Super Etendard fighters, armed with *Exocet* missiles [145]*seriously damaged a British aircraft carrier (Invincible).* This could be seen as a bit desperate on the part of the Junta after the loss of Darwin and Goose Green settlements. They may be trying to keep their public happy, which is looking increasingly doubtful. According to some reports, the Argentine people feel they may be on the verge of defeat. Sometimes, they may be able to get other news apart from Junta versions.

[146]*Argentina's papers carry huge headlines, "AIRCRAFT CARRIER INVINCIBLE BLAZING",* amongst others. This must be the most blatant piece of propaganda yet. Most likely to counter effect the bad news about Goose Green and Darwin. Invincible is still all right and in perfect working order. I can't see Galtieri lasting long if the eventual attack on Port Stanley is successful.

British frigates and destroyers again bombarded the [147]*Port Stanley airstrip.* The heaviest one yet.

---

[145] https://www.quora.com/Did-Argentina-sink-or-damage-HMS-Invincible-in-the-Falklands-War?share=1

[146] https://www.express.co.uk/news/world/977203/falklands-war-argentina-uk-hms-invincible-gerardo-isaac

[147] https://vulcantothesky.org/articles/falklands-war-1982-operation-black-buck/

Seen by the media as a softening up prior to a British attack. Argentina say they are prepared.

Latest Argentinian communique says they bombed San Carlos last night. They didn't.

Pope is visiting Britain and has said everyone should pray for peace. Point of interest: During the *Exocet* attack on us a few weeks ago, the day *Sheffield* was hit, a white dove was seen to land on our flight deck. A signal received today from Avenger, who was unsuccessfully attacked, yesterday reported a white dove landing on the fo'c's'le when the missile was sighted.

A QUIET DAY OTHERWISE.

Tuesday 1st June

[148]*British Ambassador* has given his answers to the latest UN proposals.

Argentina thinks a British attack on Port Stanley is imminent. They say they are ready with 7,000 troops, well dug in, with rockets and mortars.

Defence Ministry in London announced that 250 Argentinian troops had been killed in the fighting so far. There are also reports that a section of Argentinian troops put up a white flag.

---

[148]   https://www.telegraph.co.uk/news/obituaries/5000164/Sir-Nicholas-Henderson.html

When British troops moved into the open, they were shot.

Hospital ship *Bahia Paraiso* has picked up 170 Argentinian wounded from Port Stanley.

Quiet day so far, apart from this morning at 8 o'clock when we went to action stations. Skyhawks, Mirage and a Hercules were reported. [149] *CAP* went to intercept and shot down the Hercules plane.* No more attacks throughout day.

Attack on Port Stanley seems more imminent, maybe in the next few days. We leave San Carlos Bay tonight for a 2/3-day break to get stores and fuel onboard. We may be either joining the *Hermes* group, safe from most of the attacks, out in the TEZ, or we may proceed to the Tug Repair and Logistics Area for some essential repairs. Troops are now in control of high ground (Mount Kent).

*UK Combat Air Patrol

---

[149] http://www.naval-history.net/F64-Falklands-Argentine_aircraft_lost.htm

CHAPTER

This book mixes my own objective, historical diary observations with the media reporting of the time. The contrasts are often stark.

40 years ago, [150] Whitehall's influence over the media was seen to hold some sway. For example, if UK ships were hit or sunk, it may not have been reported immediately due to operational demands and constraints.

Now, as social media has largely swept away the old lurches to secrecy, and as foreign media proprietors have taken ownership of much of the UK press, it's become a landscape where media organisations – post [151] phone hacking, post failed [152] Levenson – have

---

[150]   https://www.fiassociation.com/article/1506/ian_mcdonald_mod_spokesman_of_the_falkland_conflict_in_1982#:~:text=his role was controversial because of the degree of censorship and control that the uk government sought to impose on the public reporting of the war%2C impossible now to achieve with the advance of satellite communications and social media

[151]   https://www.bbc.co.uk/news/uk-24894403

[152]   https://www.youtube.com/watch?v=ozQVVYry-O8

felt at liberty to act as busy, irrepressible controllers and manipulators of the content themselves. Much reported news these days is half-arsed, questionable and wreathed in ambiguity as standard.

I suspect that highly sensitive exclusives have in the past and are now being carefully drip-fed to selected, compromised outlets by Blairite / Brownite / Cameronite / Mayite / Johnsonite governments and are timed for the greatest advantage within the managed control of information. With all this mutual back scratching, no journalist exists with the ability or courage needed to blow the whistle – Assange-like – on such a sordid situation.

As regards the media and newspapers, we, as readers, viewers, listeners, taxpayers, or as servicemen and veterans have seriously [153] drawn the short straw if we're expecting to see honesty, integrity, or balanced, objective reporting.

Today, in my opinion, it's highly likely that UK track and trace systems and the monitoring of who is and isn't being 'vaccinated' will have been successfully by-passed and compromised by those who know that there's a large and booming market for people who have chosen not to be injected but who understandably don't want to lose their jobs, their personal health autonomy, their freedom to travel and maybe one day their ability to buy food and survive inside a system that continues to outrageously label itself a 'democracy'.

---

[153] https://www.independent.co.uk/news/uk/politics/revealed-jimmy-sa-vile-s-close-friendship-with-margaret-thatcher-8432351.html#:~:text=Notes on the,passed to police.

This is interesting. It's the beginnings of the 1982 post-invasion, UK parliamentary debate:

[154]*UK Hansard, Saturday 3rd April 1982, the day after the Argentine invasion.*

Wednesday 2nd June (Out in the TEZ)

[155]*News reports of thousands of gallons of Napalm found in Goose Green,* as confirmed in a signal which came in yesterday.

It was found in crudely made 220kg containers, ready for use, and fused. Napalm sticks to the skin and burns. The British finds are hotly denied by Argentina. They say the British claims are totally false. 50 tanks were found. Plus, instructions for use on a secret document. Big stink about it on the news.

Two high ranking Argentinian military officials are visiting New York to have talks with the Secretary General of the UN.

---

[154] https://hansard.parliament.uk/Commons/1982-04-03/debates/43f4bd64-426b-488d-a12e-ade282341db0/CommonsChamber#:~:text=Yesterday was,been usurped

[155] https://www.quora.com/How-many-times-did-Argentina-use-napalm-in-the-Falklands-War-and-what-units-were-targeted-by-it?share=1

News reports that Port Stanley is now under fire from ground forces on high land around the area and also under bombardment from ships. Thatcher has said there can still be an honourable withdrawal by Argentinian forces to save more bloodshed. Spain and Panama have called for a ceasefire. The British Ambassador to the US says any ceasefire would be inconsistent with [156]*Article 502 of the UN charter* which calls for Argentinian forces to leave the Falklands.

Two air raids today that didn't materialise.

Thursday 3rd June

[157]*Attempts being made to ground base GR3 Harriers* on new San Carlos airstrip. Argentine air force commander has said that the battle for Port Stanley will not be the ultimate battle in the conflict and also said he is optimistic about the outcome of the conflict.

---

[156] http://unscr.com/en/resolutions/502

[157] http://wikimapia.org/32310319/RAF-Forward-Operating-Base-San-Carlos-Site#:~:text=the airfield began regular harrier support operations on june 5th%2C 1982 when the first rn harriers landed to be refueled.

https://upload.wikimedia.org/wikipedia/commons/thumb/f/f2/Vulcan_bomber%2C_
2009_Sunderland_Airshow.jpg/640px-Vulcan_bomber%2C_2009
_Sunderland_Airshow.jpg

Thatcher has said a withdrawal of Argentinian forces would not be a humiliation but a restoration of international law.

[158]*A Vulcan bomber on an undisclosed mission* was intercepted in Brazilian airspace by two fighters. It was reported that it missed its R/V with a refuelling tanker, and it was low on fuel so had to pull into nearest airport. It was escorted into Rio de Janeiro.

British Harriers have been dropping leaflets saying that it's not worth fighting for Port Stanley. It's a ploy to persuade them to surrender without further loss of life.

---

[158]   https://www.upi.com/Archives/1982/06/03/British-bomb-er-makes-emergency-landing-in-Brazil/3327391924800/

Most of us would appreciate – 40 years on – how the whole landscape of military conflict has shifted, how western alliances have deepened, sullied themselves and how weapons and communications systems have advanced alarmingly.

Back then, although we'd voluntarily joined up, I and many of my colleagues were openly reluctant to be risking our lives 7,882 miles away. Not for the British Empire, not for [159] deeply unpopular Thatcher, not for her political party, and not for the Falkland islanders. As if to underline our reluctance, over 900 young servicemen on both sides and three female islanders ended up dead as political casualties, and many through friendly fire. It was foreseeable, avoidable, and so regrettable.

---

[159] https://www.ipsos.com/ipsos-mori/en-uk/margaret-thatcher-1925-2013#:~:text=average satisfaction with the way her government was running the country was 32%25%2C compared to an average 59%25 who were dissatisfied. the low points were 16%25 satisfied in march 1981 and again in march 1990

Fast forward to 2022 and what in 1982 was a relatively small UK-based constituency of sceptics and doubters will have mushroomed into a far larger, international one – and for good reason – in the wake of [160]*Afghanistan, Iraq, Libya, Syria, Yemen, et al. Particularly when seen against the backdrop of invasions, lies, hypocrisy, the bloody, burgeoning arms trade,* [161]*the undermining, hobbling, imprisonment and potential torture of the good souls who push for peace, and the* [162]*desperate fight or flight of stricken populations.*

<hr>

Friday 4th June

Possible air raid on British troops. Didn't occur. Held four contacts (Canberra aircraft) which turned back. Argentinians may be supplying the west island from Rio Grande airport on the mainland. *Invincible* and *Brilliant* have gone to have a look and shoot down any A/C which are found to be moving in supplies. [163]*USA have denied they were putting pressure on Britain for a ceasefire.* UN Security Council meet again soon

---

[160] https://www.youtube.com/watch?v=6fMX72z8gp8

[161] https://www.theguardian.com/australia-news/2021/dec/11/scott-morrison-urged-to-end-lunacy-and-push-us-and-uk-to-release-julian-assange

[162] https://www.aljazeera.com/news/2021/1/20/dozens-of-migrants-killed-in-shipwreck-off-the-coast-of-libya#:~:text=At least 43 migrants and refugees have been,where more than 17%2C000 have drowned since 2014.

[163] https://www.nytimes.com/1982/06/05/world/us-and-the-british-veto-resolution-on-falklands.html#:~:text=Mrs,once

to try and find a solution acceptable to both countries.

There is a possibility of Argentinian terrorist attacks on bases and stores depots at home.

We're still in the repair area, going back to join *Hermes* group at midnight, tonight. Vulcan bomber that landed at Rio is being detained at the request of Argentina. [164]*England, Scotland, and Northern Ireland are going to the World Cup after all.* Good news at last.

Saturday 5th June

[165]*USA abstained on the vote for a ceasefire.* Britain expected them to veto it.

Sunday 6th June

We're doing an NGS this morning.

03:10 Surprise, surprise – HANDS TO EMERGENCY STATIONS. FIRE IN THE BOILER ROOM UPTAKES. Everyone's gone up to the flight deck in case we have to abandon

---

[164] https://www.dailymail.co.uk/news/article-2617621/Thatchers-government-nearly-withdrew-England-Scotland-Northern-Ireland-football-teams-1982-World-Cup-case-played-Argentina-Falklands-war.html

[165] http://bufvc.ac.uk/tvandradio/lbc/index.php/segment/0012600007014

ship. I've got to stay down in the office. We were expecting action stations, not this.

03:25 It wasn't a fire but a distorted door in the funnel which was letting smoke out through the ship. Damage control parties sussing it out.

03:30 Hands to action stations for NGS. Proceeding to the gunline, close in to the coast (two miles offshore). We may come under fire from enemy shore batteries on the coast.

06:00 NGS complete.

06:05 AIR RAID WARNING RED

SURFACE WARNING RED (Two surface contacts).

06:34 HMS Cardiff is launching her Lynx to go and investigate and get visual identification.

06:50 Units are possibly friendly – closing to two miles to certify this.

07:05 Contacts established as friendly land-ing craft.

[166] *Today, over East Falkland there was a friendly fire incident involving HMS Cardiff and a 5th Brigade Gazelle helicopter*

[167] *Report of the Board of Enquiry*

[168] *Short excerpt from Falkland Islands Hansard Debate – 3rd December 1968, revealing very early concerns on the then Labour government's direction of travel.*

Monday 7th June

NOTHING.

Tuesday 8th June

02:00 Doing an NGS near Port Stanley again. Hands are at action stations.

03:30 Coming under fire from shore batteries. Close explosion starboard side. We're moving away to put a bit more range between us and them.

03:40 All blokes on the upper deck have been moved down below for safety reasons. They said

---

[166] https://www.quora.com/How-did-HMS-Cardiff-accidentally-shoot-down-a-friendly-helicopter-with-a-Sea-Dart-during-the-Falklands-War?share=1#:~:text=The Board,brigade airspace

[167] https://web.archive.org/web/20081125053424/http:/www.mod.uk/NR/rdonlyres/EF248AAE-5B25-4CB4-BE90-EE096980354B/0/boi_loss_gazellexx377.pdf

[168] https://hansard.parliament.uk/Commons/1968-12-03/debates/13b0d399-1fba-4b8b-a603-66cae54560f6/FalklandIslands#:~:text=Miss Herbison,so on

there was an explosion 100 yards away on the port side.

05:30 NGS completed. We're now safely on our way back to the *Hermes* group out in the TEZ.

Galtieri has turned down the latest UN peace initiative calling for unconditional withdrawal of Argentine troops.

17:00 (Approx)

[169]*HMS Plymouth has been hit.* She is on fire. Not sure what she was hit by, where, or if there were any casualties.

[170]*A US merchant vessel has been attacked 800 miles north of the Falklands.* It was attacked by an unidentified aircraft and is listing heavily, heading for the nearest port.

19:30 [171]*Four Mirage* came in to attack San Carlos Bay.* One LCU tank carrier hit by bomb. Two Sea Harriers intercepted them on the way out.

---

[169] http://www.naval-history.net/F53-Sir_Galahad-Sir_Tristram_bombed.htm#:~:text=First to be,only slightly damaged

[170] https://www.nytimes.com/1982/06/09/world/tanker-attacked-in-south-atlantic.html#:~:text=a 100%2C000-ton supertanker%2C bound from st. croix in the virgin islands to alaska%2C reported that it was bombed and hit by aircraft rocket fire 480 miles northeast of the falkland islands yesterday

[171] https://www.royalmarineshistory.com/post/2017/06/08/the-loss-of-royal-marines-landing-craft-lcu-f4-falklands-8th-june-1982#:~:text=at 16%3A50 a second wave%2C composed of four a-4bs skyhawks hit and sank f4 a landing craft utility from hms fearless in choiseul sound.

Leader shot down two Mirage. Second Harrier shot down third Mirage and the fourth Mirage collided into the debris or lost control and crashed into sea. Pilot managed to eject, and his chute was seen to open.

These were later identified as Argentine Skyhawks.

HMS Plymouth had five casualties, one serious. Not clear how badly she was hit. Two A/C were shot down in the raid (one by *Plymouth*'s *Seacat*). Bluff Cove and Fitzroy settlements captured by British troops. These are very close to the main garrison at Port Stanley.

[172]*RFA Sir Galahad and RFA Sir Tristram* (landing craft carriers) were bombed today. British casualties were said to be heavier than at first thought.

[173]*There was a detachment of Welsh Guards onboard Sir Galahad* which was hit by bombs and had a lot of ammunition onboard.

Argentines have said a British frigate was sunk (*HMS Plymouth* was damaged). More propaganda?

---

[172] https://www.youtube.com/watch?v=QLw5HDjc7zs
[173] https://forcesreunited.wordpress.com/2013/06/08/the-bombing-of-sir-galahad/comment-page-1/

Wednesday 9th June

No statement released yet about casualties on *RFA Sir Galahad* or *RFA Sir Tristram*. We've got an NGS tonight at Mount Harriet. A QUIET DAY.

CHAPTER

14

RFAs Sir Tristram and Sir Galahad were crowded with personnel. They both caught fire and were quickly abandoned. The casualties for Sir Galahad were catastrophic, with a total of 48 killed; five RFA crewmen, 32 Welsh Guards and 11 other Army personnel, with many others badly burned.

* * * * * *

[174]*Detailed timeline to the invasion of the Falkland Islands in April 1982 by Russell Phillips. This crib sheet helps us trace the duplicitous conduct of Thatcher and her ministers. Much of the information around this was deliberately hidden from the public until 2012.*

Being deeply sceptical and hostile towards the person issuing my orders at the time of the conflict – right through to her fall from power – one way to dissociate myself from her and to try (and fail) to validate my service to family and friends was to stress

---

[174]   https://russellphillips.uk/timeline-to-invasion-falklands-1982/

the admittedly trifling part I'd played in opposing [175]Nixon and Kissinger's deadly Operation Condor and Dirty War in Argentina and elsewhere across South and Central America, of which Galtieri was a major proponent. Thatcher never considered criticising these crimes for one moment. I did.

[176]There was heroic opposition inside Argentina, but to her shame, [177]Thatcher had never publicly acknowledged the disappearances, nor taken the USA, Argentina or Chile to task on them. I'm drawn to conclude the murders and secret burials must have been what she'd wanted all along, making her a willing associate to these crimes.

Worse still, she'd developed [178]very close, unsavoury ties to Chilean war criminal Pinochet, who from the start was involved in torturing, killing, and disappearing his own people. Even before necrophiliac child rapist [179]Jimmy Savile came onto the scene, Thatcher was stained by her associations, and was never able to boast a clean conscience, much less, any wholesome side to her character.

---

[175] https://medium.com/exploring-history/operation-condor-u-s-and-lat-in-americas-dirty-war-d59a7cfff77c#:~:text=the thought of another communist government in latin america%2C specially at the height of the cold war%2C was anathema to current u.s. president richard nixon and henry kissinger.

[176] https://en.wikipedia.org/wiki/Adolfo_Pérez_Esquivel

[177] https://hansard.parliament.uk/Commons/1982-05-20/debates/e348886e-0a6a-486a-b54d-dcc1c6b1122f/FalklandIslands?highlight=tam nuclear#:~:text=i wish that he were not almost a lone voice on the conservative benches making such denunciations.

[178] https://newsimg.bbc.co.uk/1/hi/uk_politics/467114.stm

[179] https://www.youtube.com/watch?v=O4Lv2zJG25k&t=476s

More fool me for joining the British Empire's forces in 1976, you could say and I couldn't begin to argue with that. How naive of me as a boy! At least I'd had the foresight to grab three years of relative mental calm before this ambitious political titan roared onto the scene.

From my vantage point, as a thinking serviceman and later a veteran, the sooner you arrive at the safe conclusion that you've been ill-advised or even conned, and you regret what you did, the quicker you'll find yourself in a position to minimise any potential damage accruing to your own mental health.

———— ✦✦✦✦ ————

So, who was behind [180] the 1979 Defence Review and the wide-ranging [181] defence cuts? Step forward Margaret H. Thatcher, who'd placed trade links, a ceding of sovereignty, and future co-operation with Argentina well ahead of the wishes of the Falkland Islanders. This conduct was a far cry from her wartime claim, "The British government regards the right of the islanders to [182] self-determination as paramount."

Actions speak far, far louder than words.

[180]   https://www.fiassociation.com/article/1037/lord_carrington#:~:text=The 1979,with Argentina.

[181]   https://www.theguardian.com/uk/2011/dec/30/thatcher-warned-defence-cuts-falklands

[182]   https://scholar.smu.edu/cgi/viewcontent.cgi?article=2716&context=til

---

Thursday 10th June

NGS completed. Many enemy casualties reported. Equipment on fire. Attack on Port Stanley is planned for tonight 11th / 12th June. Much air activity reported near Argentinian coastline. Probably pilots training.

A QUIET DAY AGAIN.

Friday 11th June

[183]*We have an NGS along with four other ships tonight.* Probably the most dangerous mission yet assigned to us. We will be backing up 42 Commando as they attack Argentinian positions on Mt Harriet.

Tonight, three Falkland Islands civilians were killed by the 'friendly fire' of this bombardment. Nobody will ever know which of the five ships involved caused these civilian deaths. The part I played in this and all the other Naval Gunfire Support missions – which will have killed and injured many Argentinian volunteers and conscripts – was the setting up and testing of the radio circuits. These were used for our ship to communicate over the airwaves with shore-based Army spotters who would guide the ship's 4.5-inch shellfire onto enemy positions. I was culpable, and I regret obeying these orders.

---

[183] https://www.globalsecurity.org/military/library/report/1986/WDG.
htm#:~:text=Privacy,Pike

[184] *The civilians killed were apparently together at the same location; Susan Whitley, 30, Doreen Bonner, 36, and Mary Goodwin, 82.*

⋯✦✦✦⋯

Saturday 12th June

[185] *With HMS Glamorgan and HMS Avenger on gunline.*

02:01 Troops have started the advance on Port Stanley.

02:19 Shoreside fighting has commenced with first contact being made.

02:30 Troops working their way through booby traps.

02:40 Some prisoners taken.

02:45 Assault is going well with objectives being taken early.

02:51 Hand to hand fighting is taking place. One friendly casualty so far.

---

[184] https://sama82.org.uk/timeline-june/#:~:text=killed in action%3Amrs doreen bonnermrs mary goodwinmrs susan whitley

[185] https://www.independent.co.uk/news/obituaries/admiral-sir-hugo-white-commander-who-fought-exocet-attacks-during-falklands-war-and-was-later-governor-gibraltar-9588010.html#:~:text=woodward assigned avenger and arrow%2C with the frigate yarmouth and the destroyer glamorgan%2C to support the land forces with naval bombardment

03:06 We have been firing for a while and have reports that our shells have taken out a 120mm gun position.

03:10 The ship is under fire from enemy positions on the coast.

03:12 Firing seems to be effective. No more enemy activity at present. Many enemy dead reported.

03:20 Advance continuing. Four 120mm guns captured, along with ammunition.

03:25 Troops have asked for continuous fire to back up advance of second sub-unit (Scots Guards).

03:30 Second major sub-unit now crossing start-line and heading towards their objective.

04:15 Ships here may come under a hostile air attack soon.

04:20 Second sub-unit have contact with the enemy.

04:21 Second sub-unit attacking with mortar fire.

04:45 Friendly CAP on station for the air raid from the west

05:07 First sub-unit (45 Commando marines) have secured their objective (Mount Harriet).

Second sub-unit (3 Para) moving up hill on their objective.

05:25 45 Commando have taken and secured their position. 3 Para moving into second objective but being pinned down by sniper fire.

06:00 Clearing up last pockets of resistance now.

06:03 Enemy helicopters reported landing and dropping off troops behind our lines. More NGS requested.

06:07 NGS not now required. Don't know what's happening with the helicopters.

06:15 We're leaving the area now.

06:36 POSSIBLE *EXOCET* ATTACK. CHAFF FIRED.

06:38 Contact coming towards us (fast). Probable *Exocet*. Everyone on the floor (kiss your arse goodbye?)

06:40 Glamorgan appears to have been [186]*hit by an Exocet*. She is hit aft. She fired a *Seacat* at the missile but missed it. Still waiting for a report from the *Glamorgan*.

06:42 We are closing in on *Glamorgan* to give assistance. *Avenger* is also coming.

---

[186] https://www.youtube.com/watch?v=1zvJZe4jd_o

07:05 Glamorgan has a major fire aft. She said she doesn't need any assistance at present. We're half a mile away, ready to move in if required. She's still got propulsion (doing 15 knots).

07:30 Proceeding back to *Hermes* group with *Glamorgan* in company. They will send out Harrier A/C to cover us as we are more vulnerable at this speed.

08:00 Nothing on the news about the successful advance on Port Stanley or the *Glamorgan* incident.

12:00 [187] *Casualties from Glamorgan: 12 dead, 16 injured*, (one seriously, both legs amputated). The injuries are bad again. Flight crew and cooks suffered the most. Eye injuries, broken arms and legs, smoke inhalation, cuts, and shock. *Glamorgan*'s Wessex helicopter was disintegrated. The missile went in through the flight deck (unusual for an *Exocet*).

20:00 News is out about the British advance. No news about *Glamorgan* yet.

23:00 Still no news on *Glamorgan*.

---

[187]   https://www.walesonline.co.uk/news/wales-news/hms-glamorgans-casualties-honoured-long-1851130

> **Sunday 13th June**
>
> *00:01* No news on Glamorgan. Argentines say they sank a frigate last night. Ministry of Defence have said nothing yet. Pope has finished his visit to Argentina. Told them all to pray for peace. NGS tonight again.

Today, the morale amongst HMS Yarmouth's communicators reached a new low. On the domestic front, I was browbeaten into officially disciplining one of my favourite starboard watch colleagues, who'd failed to tidy and mop out the mess deck after coming off watch on Sunday morning. I think he blamed me. But I blame the pain in the arse Petty Officer Radio Supervisor who was forever on my case for being 'far too forgiving' with the fellas on my watch.

[188] *On the evening of Sunday 13th June John Nott made a statement on HMS Glamorgan and the Fitzroy bombings.*

---

[188]   https://www.youtube.com/watch?v=MK0cMrtOYlE

CHAPTER

15

In the lead up to the invasion, why did Thatcher seek to decommission the hydrographic, scientific survey vessel HMS Endurance against the [189] wishes of Lord Carrington, [190] Admiral Sir Henry Leach and the Falkland Islanders? Why was the Prime Minister privately pro-Argentine sovereignty and trade, and publicly [191] against granting full British citizenship to the islanders? In the months

LRO Paul

---

[189] https://www.fiassociation.com/article/1037/lord_carrington#:~:text=Assessment-,As Foreign Secretary%2C Lord,initially%2C from Mrs Thatcher).,-It was a

[190] https://www.huffingtonpost.co.uk/2011/12/29/margaret-thatcher-iron-lady-falklands_n_1174020.html#:~:text=Margaret Thatcher was,rule show how

[191] https://www.legislationline.org/download/id/5951/file/British_nationality_act_am2003_en.pdf

leading up to the conflict, what kind of signal did this appeasement send to the Argentine junta? That any subsequent Argentine invasion was unlikely to be challenged? That would be the most likely conclusion to arrive at.

From the Argentine newspapers: [192] *"Britain is thereby abandoning the protection of the Falkland Islands."*

It's clear to me that the unstated cause of this conflict – concealed for 30 years – was the secret activity around ceding Falklands sovereignty, all closely linked to the future military, strategic and trade interests of Britain and Argentina. According to certain autumn 1980 [193] *secret documents, a realisation was dawning on Thatcher that sovereignty could not be passed to the military junta this time around and that the islands could not be leased back to Argentina for 99 years, as Nicholas Ridley had fervently wished. At such a crucial stage in the long-term process, why did Thatcher's priority switch to taking a sharpened axe to the UK's presence in the South Atlantic?*

If an Argentine invasion was being considered, encouraged, or even actively precipitated, there could never be any traceable contact in this regard between the British and Argentine governments. This would immediately indicate collusion, and would have risked discovery, betrayal, later exposure, or the collapse of the Thatcher government. There is a telling quote in the above document: "…complete secrecy was essential to both

---

[192]   http://fc95d419f4478b3b6e5f-3f71d0fe2b653c4f00f32175760e96e7.
        r87.cf1.rackcdn.com/1703B13AA0CD43E5B5225176CC5720A6.pdf
[193]   https://c59574e9047e61130f13-3f71d0fe2b653c4f00f32175760e96e7.
        ssl.cf1.rackcdn.com/BAD0573864714A95838DC583BF8C50C0.pdf

sides". If Thatcher's hidden wish was to be re-elected to power at all costs in June 1983, she could drop heavy hints in the form of positive ongoing trade talks, the ceding of sovereignty, swingeing UK defence cuts, [194] the removal of HMS Endurance from service, etc. to imply to Galtieri that an Argentine invasion would stand uncontested, whilst quietly factoring in the surmountable, 'acceptable' cost of a large, but unknown number of expendable servicemen's lives on both sides. As it turned out, the defence cuts, trade talks, proposals for the ceding of sovereignty and clandestine meetings with the Argentine government were exactly what she carried out – [195] amid howls of protest from senior military figures. As I've referred to time and again, the full details of these were kept under wraps for 30 years.

Between the early 1970s and today, I've felt a deep mistrust of unscrupulous political players like Thatcher, the alleged 'free' press and media, and a huge, burgeoning shitstorm of local authority [196] Rotten Boroughs, stuffed with broken humans. This scandalous conduct has been around for so long, many of us feel like we've become virtually marinated in it.

My deep misgivings occurred to me firstly as a schoolboy, continued later as a sailor, developed further as a civilian

---

[194] https://hansard.parliament.uk/Lords/1981-06-30/debates/1c0a9643-ff36-494a-8897-a99f5206bc2f/TheFalklandIslandsSovereignty#:~:text=I am disturbed,possibly come about.
[195] https://penpointreview.blogspot.com/2011/12/records-reveal-thatchers-defence-cuts.html#:~:text=The files also,them%2C
[196] https://www.youtube.com/watch?v=zSYAqZeMqTQ

employee, [197] and have been evolving in my semi-retirement. What started initially as a gap in trust has become a yawning gulf. We are where we are, and as the situation has deteriorated, [198] I find I'm never going to mellow with age, as so many do. Who is there left to trust? Apart from friends, family, [199] Julian Assange, [200] Edward Snowden, [201] Craig Murray, [202] John Pilger and [203] Declassified UK (list not exhaustive), nobody, it seems. The silence of mainstream journalists on the Assange and Murray causes célèbres is extremely telling. My own doubts have grown, as I've watched a procession of shameless liars become more brazen, as they pick their moment to creep out of the woodwork. At the same time, more innocent civilians, and more young forces men and [204] women continue to lose their lives so cheaply. The professed democratic checks and balances of old have perished as lambs to the slaughter, to the point where freedom of the press now finds itself laid out on the sacrificial altar, and [205] UK publishers and journalists face being arrested, tried, and locked up, simply for doing their jobs.

---

[197] https://www.youtube.com/watch?v=XuNhRO820_s

[198] https://www.youtube.com/watch?v=tV9PX8LM83w

[199] https://www.independent.co.uk/topic/julian-assange

[200] https://www.amnesty.org.uk/edward-snowden-nsa-whistleblower-pardon

[201] https://wirralinittogether.blog/2021/11/30/journalist-craig-murray-released-from-prison-craigs-speech-craigmurrayfreeagain/

[202] https://www.youtube.com/watch?v=zH8cNGQ4Khs

[203] https://www.youtube.com/c/DeclassifiedUK

[204] https://www.express.co.uk/news/uk/1518361/army-news-military-careers-women

[205] https://inforrm.org/2021/07/22/official-secrets-act-home-secretarys-planned-reform-will-make-criminals-out-of-journalists-karin-wahl-jorgensen/

Monday 14ᵗʰ June

01:59 Troops have started advancing.

02:00 Commenced firing for this morning's NGS. We're on our own at the moment, waiting for three others to arrive later on. We're firing in support of the Scots Guards. Troops are going well, meeting no opposition at present. Earlier on, *Cardiff* splashed one A/C. Shore-based *Rapiers* claimed another one. The remainder of the air raids opened out to the west.

02:20 Leading elements are pushing forward. [206]*Spotter* reports that first objective should be no problem.

03:40 Two objectives taken already. Scots Guards now attacking Tumbledown Hill. But they're being pinned down by sniper-fire at present. Enemy are taking cover behind rocks on the higher ground. Spotter has directed our fire further up the hill, pushing the enemy upwards. Very effective firing reported.

06:00 We've got to leave now as it will be light soon. Don't know whether they've secured Tumbledown Hill.

---

[206] https://military.wikia.org/wiki/Artillery_observer

07:30 Hands fall out of action stations. We should be okay now. On our way back to Carrier Battle Group. We should have another NGS tonight. They'll probably send us in as much as possible as they've got

big supplies of MK6 ammunition. Hopefully, they'll keep us away from the *Exocet* danger area.

13:00 News: [207]*Peru may have been supplying Argentina with Exocet missiles.* The missiles were sent to Peru from Aerospatiale in France before the conflict started.

14:00 News about the *Glamorgan* is out. Nine known to have been killed. Four missing, presumed dead (these four must have been in the

area of the impact) and 15 injured. Troops have been continuing the advance throughout the day.

15:35 Heard on NGS radio circuit: "Paras will soon be marching into Port Stanley and an enemy surrender looks imminent."

15:55 Heard on NGS radio circuit: [208]*"WHITE FLAGS FLYING OVER STANLEY."* The news of a ceasefire was heard on the news

[207] https://www.margaretthatcher.org/source/prem19/prem19-0649#:~:-text=Su-,declassified documents,-Key*Exocet* missiles
[208] https://en.mercopress.com/2002/11/12/white-flags-over-stanley

tonight. [209]*Thatcher announced to the House of Commons* that the surrender was being negotiated. Argentines are looking for an honourable way out of the conflict. Total British killed reported as 250. Total Argentines killed reported as 750 (approx.).

21:35 An English-speaking Argentine came up on the NGS net. He said, *"EVEN THOUGH YOU THINK YOU HAVE WON THIS WAR OVER THE MALVINAS, SOME DAY WE ARE GOING TO RETURN AND KICK THE BRITISH OUT, EVEN THOUGH YOU THINK IT IS OVER."*

23:00 BBC World Service news report that a ceasefire is now in force. But the Argentinians have not surrendered yet. Menendez, the Argentine commander on the Falklands, is on his way to Argentina to have talks with Galtieri.

---

[209] https://hansard.parliament.uk/Commons/1982-06-15/debates/39c162f7-da2b-4e6e-a42d-1e90c67a1901/FalklandIslands#:~:text=the texts of all the negotiations are not mine to publish. we entered into the negotiations in confidence and i do not believe in breaking a confidence.

CHAPTER

16

Before the Argentine invasion, the Thatcher government had set out its stall, taking several direct actions and making numerous public statements, all confirming our suspicions they weren't interested in keeping the Falkland Islands British.

Thatcher – who feigned such close affinity for the Falkland Islanders during the conflict – had already singled them out beforehand, ensuring they were downgraded to "non-British" status in her [210]British Nationality Act 1981, which meant not only Falkland Islanders, but several other cast-offs of empire [211]would have no right to live in the UK and would be treated as foreigners.

---

[210] https://www.legislationline.org/download/id/5951/file/British_nationality_act_am2003_en.pdf

[211] https://russellphillips.uk/timeline-to-invasion-falklands-1982/#:~:text=october 1981%3A the british nationality act 1981 receives royal assent. the act removes british citizenship from most falkland islanders%2C removing their right to live in the uk.

But Thatcher's driving hypocrisy was the stuff of legend. After the conflict, in a carefully timed electioneering move, she passed an amendment to the Act, granting the Falkland Islanders full British citizenship:

> 1.0.0.3. The second addition is set out in s.1(1) of the British Nationality (Falkland Islands) Act 1983 passed on **28 March 1983**. This provides that a person who on 1 January 1983 became a British Dependent Territories citizen under s.23 of the British Nationality Act 1981 also became on that date a British citizen...

This separate legislation gave the Falkland Islanders their new status just two short years after her uncompromising refusal to grant it had been cemented in, supposedly 'for good'. It arrived two months before the June 1983 election. This screeching U-turn would never have occurred without the conflict, the 907 deaths and the increasingly likely return of a UK Conservative government.

---

[212]Prior to the war, on the 10th and 11th September 1980, with lucrative trade deals in mind, British Foreign Office Minister Nicholas Ridley and Lord Chalfont held secret negotiations

---

[212] https://en.wikipedia.org/wiki/Falkland_Islands#:~:text=From 1966,passing time

with the fascist Argentine junta, [213] discussed sovereignty and sought closer ties to Argentina. Grave concerns were raised by Falkland islanders over the potential loss of UK sovereignty, but Ridley waved them away. He'd been dead for 12 years when this crucial part of the official war narrative finally emerged in 2005. By then it was too late to make anybody answer for it.

---

[214] Operation Algeciras – Rarely discussed by UK government and media – who were rightly embarrassed – this failed, clandestine attack on UK ships in Gibraltar was conceived, ordered, and directly managed by Argentine Admiral – and the man behind thousands of civilian disappearances – [215] Jorge Anaya.

---

[213] https://www.theguardian.com/uk/2005/jun/28/falklands.past

[214] https://en.wikipedia.org/wiki/Operation_Algeciras

[215] https://en.wikipedia.org/wiki/Jorge_Anaya

CHAPTER

17

LRO Paul

Since World War II the UK has been all but umbilically connected to the [216] United States. Across an 80-year sweep of time, geopolitical changes have ebbed and flowed around a significant number of far-reaching, ultra-offensive, western military campaigns, where the UK seems to have tagged along as an obedient also-ran. I've felt my own perspectives shifting, but there's been one steady constant which persists to this day; the recruiting sergeant sells dreams but delivers nightmares.

---

[216] https://off-guardian.org/2021/11/28/us-terrorism-101-the-bert-sacks-story/

Impressionable youngsters, targeted and absorbed from largely working-class families, continue to be drawn in, put through their paces, indoctrinated, mentally harmed, or maimed for life. Occasionally they will end up perishing on a lie. Few emerge from active service as they went in, unharmed.

For precisely what in return did the hundreds of dead soldiers, sailors, an airman and three civilians make the ultimate sacrifice? Largely, we're told it was to salvage this tiny population's British pride over land they never owned, along with their major industry; some economically tanking [217]sheep farming, the vast majority of which was carried out on rented land.

There was a Falkland Islands population of just 1,847 in 1982. Roughly speaking, for every two liberated islanders, a British or Argentine forces member gave up his life.

For every UK armed force member involved in the conflict, 15.4 Falkland Island sheep were provided with salvation.

The farming of this rented land had for centuries been the traditional way of life for the Falkland Islanders; a harsh, hard-fought existence they were so desperate to preserve and protect from the Argentine incursion. This was their principal occupation and a huge element of the 'paramount interests' quoted ad nauseum by Thatcher.

---

[217] https://en.wikipedia.org/wiki/Economy_of_the_Falkland_Is-
lands#:~:text=By the Falklands War of 1982 sheep farming was the
islands' only industry%5B3%5D and their economic viability was in
doubt%2C

As history now sees it, these new on the scene, much flaunted 'paramount' interests – which hadn't been evident before and seem to have been conjured up in 1982 – were the prime justification for 255 young British servicemen and three Falkland Islanders having their lives cut short.

Whoever did the pre-war cost / benefit analysis, before concluding it was worth our while venturing most of the way across the planet to recover a small number of anonymous UK landlords' frozen, windswept property – along with their tenants – must have been either living in cloud cuckoo land, or acting fully in keeping with a concealed, party-political agenda.

I would suggest the former AND the latter.

Today, it appears the Falkland Islanders' long-cherished, traditional farming economy is being abandoned [218] and very soon, into its place will flow dirty oil and gas. Or at least, that's the plan. It's notable how the tiny, and now somewhat credulous FIG (Falkland Islands Government) – which speaks in glowing terms of a 'burgeoning oil industry' – only succeeds in [219] reducing itself even further in stature and divesting itself of all integrity.

<hr />

To the old, hard of thinking conservative jingoist – who doesn't know one end of an SA80A3 from the other – it doesn't matter if the enemy's a 55-year-old hard-bitten general or a 16-year-old,

---

[218]   https://www.falklands.gov.fk/self-sufficiency/commercial-sectors/oil/
[219]   https://www.washingtonpost.com/climate-environment/2021/12/13/thwaites-glacier-melt-antarctica/

wet behind the ears cadet. It's [220] our boys' opportunity to shine. The enemy shall die before we do.

And if our boys are killed, they died for their country – whichever blood-smeared, gun-running set-up that happens to be – with something referred to as 'honour'. But seriously, what sort of an achievement can it ever be to make like a bullet-ridden corpse, after being cut down in your prime of life on the orders of some dishonest, posturing, ambitious politician?

UK and Argentine politicians stitched us all up, sent us to war, whipped up nationalistic fervour, appealed to patriotism, lit the blue touchpaper, retired to a safe distance, then sat back to munch on popcorn and watch the spectacle. Soon, with the dead forgotten, they were loving the plaudits and counting the June 1983 votes as they flooded in.

They'd enjoyed the luxury of plenty of time to plot and think their options through.

But how many active, fighting men had the same time to think and weigh their options as death came racing towards them? Once you're there where the bullets and missiles fly, the time you spend thinking is the time you get killed in.

The war-dead, strewn across a field, or sunk to the ocean bed all look alike because death is a great leveller. It's a cliché, but generals, privates, kings, beggars, all are rendered equal when they're lying in the mud. 'The fallen' – or the blown up, the decapitated, the drowned, the vapourised – are remembered as

---

[220]   https://youtu.be/3JZlP5qQVtE?t=334

courageous, God-fearing, armed forces patriots, proud to have sacrificed themselves and – strangely – will always be remembered clad in their uniforms.

The statues of proud soldiers, sailors and airmen in military dress are the public-facing result of carefully thought out, ongoing, well-practised manipulation. Otherwise known as cynical, calculated fakery.

The truth for most is they were scared human beings, dressed in the uniform of empire, but who'd become deceased via the whims of powerful, exploitative others; interfering rogues who'd hoodwinked them into service, then played havoc with their hopes and dreams before dispensing with them, leaving their families to grieve. They'd then carved their figures out in stone or bronze, and as a cynical afterthought, always draped them in their combats.

To end up dying for a squalid government you could never respect, nor revere is the crushing height of folly. In this regard, the sheer depths of my own relief remain unfathomable 40 years later.

In their headlong pursuit of power and influence, the practised psychopaths seated on top of the military industrial pyramid have left a long trail of corpses in their wake. They never pause to look back, around, or where they came from.

<hr>

Neither do they get their hands dirty fighting. Through blind, unthinking arrogance and bloodlust, they're at liberty to

117

squander more lives on all sides, and to dodge or obliterate each peace threatening 'obstacle' as it blocks their path.

The utilitarian notion of the 'greater good' is scant consolation to those about to be sacrificed in its name, which never happens to be those eagerly pushing the idea. The anonymous shits who occupy the shadows whilst backing armed conflict – all failed excuses for human beings – would sooner pick an easy war than be forced into carving out a difficult peace.

I emerged from this conflict as a man with high hopes and fingers crossed for a peaceful, more secure existence:

> ➢ A world turning with a purpose and promising us all a brighter future.
> ➢ A world that could produce courageous figureheads, fired up and ready to eke out [221]a genuine, attainable peace
> ➢ A world that could learn from the mistakes, stand proud and move forward, neither glorifying nor celebrating past conquests
> ➢ A world that could respectfully remember the war dead, grasp the opportunity to learn lessons and stop adding to their numbers
> ➢ A world where we could defend ourselves effectively and honestly when called for, and not pre-emptively, under false pretexts or phantom threats

---

[221] https://www.lewrockwell.com/2021/09/david-gordon/should-war-be-made-humane/

> *A world of opportunity, one that could deliver safe, harmonious, prosperous times for everybody, including our children and all who come after us.*

None of this was permitted to happen. The subsequent carnage, plunder and sacrificing of thousands of young lives on an altar of fake patriotism is not working.

⁺⁺⁺⁺⁺⁺⁺

In the year 2022, have the recruiting sergeants grasped and delivered our dreams, [222] or just the same old nightmares? I've witnessed little progress in all this time and currently, the hope for a new era of robust, genuine defence, no more permanent wars and no more proliferation of far-flung military bases seems like a distant pipedream.

Meanwhile the dead eyed, 11th November phantoms, when not busy with their latest PR stunt, will soon be along to haunt us again, queueing for their chance to publicly tarnish the memory of thousands of lost, largely working-class forces members. Heedless of the living and bereft of life themselves, this bunch of damaged, shuffling ghouls are drawn to the same, easy photo opportunity every year. They disgust me and if you're an honest, dignified human being, you should be disgusted too.

---

[222] https://nationalinterest.org/blog/reboot/russia-still-worries-about-nato-invasion-and-here's-why-196591

[223]*June 1981. Lord Buxton of Alsa – On Thatcher's 'horrifying prospect'; a package of defence cuts and the planned decommissioning of* [224]*British survey vessel HMS Endurance, the UK's only presence in the South Atlantic; "Our long-term interest in the resources of the South Atlantic will be placed in serious jeopardy". So, this was a rare example of publicly expressed regret over a loss of opportunity, re: distant resources. How revealing.*

[223] https://hansard.parliament.uk/Lords/1981-06-30/debates/1c0a9643-ff36-494a-8897-a99f5206bc2f/TheFalklandIslandsSovereignty#:~:-text=I am disturbed,represent British interests

[224] https://hansard.parliament.uk/Lords/1981-06-30/debates/1c0a9643-ff36-494a-8897-a99f5206bc2f/TheFalklandIslandsSovereignty#:~:-text=I outlined,come about.

MARGARET
THATCHER
1925-2013

Thatcher and Galtieri's rousing, far-flung 1982 face-off was a controlled show. One for which the participating nations and other interested countries had been waiting several decades. When the balloon finally went up, impatient arms dealers and senior military figures got what they'd been craving; the green light to let fly – for real – with the latest tested, but unproven weapons.

[225]*Powerful, vested interests were served as weapons markets received a massive shot in the arm. How much more proof do we need that merciless, uncaring, unadulterated greed is an ever-present influence?*

In discussion the following points were made:-

a.   It should be possible to apply pressure on Spain to take a less hostile public position, eg at the United Nations, since she was an important trading partner and needed British support for entry into the European Community.   But the Spanish Government's attitude was more moderate in private;   and Britain had important interests at stake in the opening of the Gibraltar frontier due on 25 June and in the Anglo-Spanish talks scheduled to start simultaneously.

b.   There was likely to be Parliamentary concern about the supply of arms and military equipment to Argentina from Israel and from South Africa.   There was no doubt that a substantial quantity of Israeli military equipment was reaching Argentina through third countries.

SECRET

Both leaders were Machiavellian to the core. He craved and won his brief boost in popularity but squandered his freedom. She craved and won her war but squandered the beckoning peace. A peace that was constantly on offer and within her grasp. A peace that would have saved 900+ lives but won no elections.

Thatcher's callous machinations – [226]*like the sinking of the Belgrano when a peace deal was waiting on the table – and*

---

225   https://www.independent.co.uk/news/world/middle-east/israel-sold-weapons-argentina-falklands-war-declassified-files-foreign-office-a7209646.html

226   https://www.lrb.co.uk/the-paper/v06/n06/tam-dalyell/tam-dalyell-on-the-sunday-sinking-of-the-belgrano

her subsequent lies, were always geared towards a particular and sordid end, the manipulation of hearts, minds and public opinion on a grand scale, and the renewal and consolidation of her own power, done at any cost.

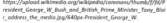

https://upload.wikimedia.org/wikipedia/commons/thumb/f/fd/President_George_W_Bush_and_British_Prime_Minister_Tony_Blair_address_the_media.jpg/640px-President_George_W.

https://upload.wikimedia.org/wikipedia/commons/thumb/a/ab/Shock-awe-graffiti.jpg/640px-Shock-awe-graffiti.jpg

Bloodline [227] Bush and Bawbag [228] Blair arrived much later, as we all know. Two shrunken, trigger-happy war addicts, polished in image, but soiled in character. Hawking the same twisted ideologies, brash and belligerent, they were practically born to the cause of delivering pain and death on an unimaginable scale. Crucially, the immediate era post 9/11 was a key staging post. Stunted in compassion and with zero humanitarian insight, they could neither meet the challenge nor grasp the opportunity provided by the strategic deck of cards that had been laid before them.

---

[227] https://wirralinittogether.blog/2020/12/31/our-next-round-is-dedicated-to-the-us-president-george-w-bush-uk-panel-game-im-sorry-i-havent-a-clue-has-fun-with-the-former-potus-this-is-hilarious/

[228] https://www.telesurenglish.net/news/5-Facts-About-the-War-Criminal-Tony-Blair-20160705-0031.html

This was the perfect time for calm, thoughtful deliberation via international diplomacy. Instead, they tore straight into satisfying their own depraved impulses. Both administrations spurned every chance for mature dialogue, and instead – on a false pretext – lurched into a relentless terror offensive from which the world has yet to emerge. Their many successors have brought nothing to the table, compounding the suffering of millions.

In the lead up to the Iraq War, these callous puppets ignored massive public protest and ploughed on regardless. Pretty soon, as expected, the same dismal bells were heard tolling again. The civilian deaths that resulted were horrendous and had all been carried out illegally. Eventually, [229]up to 2.4 million Iraqis lay dead.

The onus for the dirty work had once again been placed onto low-ranking servicemen, who obeyed orders, cranked up the vicious attacks and risked their own lives bailing out the errant trash at the top. If they survived, once again, they'd be cast to one side, [230]and most likely left to deal with any PTSD or [231]government inflicted chronic health issues alone and unsupported.

Thanks to Bush and Blair, there came a sudden, unforeseen, freefall plunge in the UK's reputation. We could no longer boast fair treatment of captive personnel. The stockpile of assumed

---

[229]   https://www.mintpressnews.com/iraq-and-beyond-how-many-millions-have-been-killed-in-american-wars/239468/

[230]   https://www.mirror.co.uk/news/uk-news/ministry-defence-denies-compensation-1000-25561583

[231]   https://thevaccinereaction.org/2017/04/the-anthrax-vaccine-and-gulf-war-illness/

'good repute' was frittered away as [232]*a new version of third world-style barbarity got dragged out into the open.*

Blighty, in league with Uncle Sam, had been exposed as tor-turers. [233]*"Enhanced Interrogation Techniques" was the chilling euphemism for this new and sickening take on human savagery. Such cruel and retrograde steps had now become* [234]*a cowardly new frontier on how to inflict harm. This Geneva Convention-busting conduct was justified by the assertion; 'we need to extract intelligence' - which often led to* [235]*fake confessions, the arrests of innocents and yet more torture.*

Iraq blighted,
Villain knighted,
What a travesty,
Your bloody Majesty.

It eventually became clear to everyone that Bush's and Blair's high, polished portfolios concealed low, sordid ambitions. Now, in 2022, we're cautioned that the world has never been more unsafe, more uncertain and we've never been under such a high level of threat. If true, why is that? Because after 20 years of ir-repressible bloodletting, plunder and grinding neo-colonialism, with no end in sight, endless wars and a far more dangerous

---

[232] https://www.theguardian.com/uk/2009/feb/23/binyam-mo-hamed-guantanamo-plane-lands

[233] https://www.humanrightsfirst.org/sites/default/files/Enhanced-Inter-rogation-Fact-Sheet.pdf

[234] https://declassifieduk.org/abduction-and-denial-the-uks-role-in-torture/

[235] https://wrongful-convictions.blogspot.com/2009/05/tor-ture-and-false-confessions.html

world were always the inevitable outcomes. All sold to us on a ticket of 'defence'.

Defence?
[236] *The UK has 145 military bases in 42 countries*

REVEALED: THE UK MILITARY'S OVERSEAS BASE NETWORK INVOLVES 145 SITES IN 42 COUNTRIES

Britain's armed forces have a far more extensive base network than ever presented by the Ministry of Defence. New research by Declassified reveals the extent of this global military presence for the first time – as the government announces an extra 10% spending on defence.

Defence?
[237] *The UK is involved in seven separate covert wars around the world.*

---

[236] https://en.wikipedia.org/wiki/Overseas_military_bases_of_the_United_Kingdom
[237] https://www.youtube.com/watch?v=LFpIa8GnyOg

BRITAIN'S SEVEN COVERT WARS: AN EXPLAINER

The United Kingdom is fighting at least seven covert wars largely outside parliamentary or democratic oversight.

MARK CURTIS AND MATT KENNARD
16 SEPTEMBER 2019

An admiral points to a union flag on a screen. It marks a location which is largely unknown to the public he serves. A prime minister stood next to him smiles and slides a bottle towards him. "Well done my good man. [238]*Pull the pin and take a shot of this British Legion rum. That distant dot is still ours."*

◆◆◆◆◆

With £17 million of UK taxpayer funds invested in its defence annually, the distant dot of the Falkland Islands may soon become a maintained and protected anachronism, a 21st Century, fossil fuelled, fortress economy.

[239]*Since 2015 it's been* [240]*seeking to embrace oil and gas and to push economic ideas that are not just heavily at odds with*

---

238 https://www.civilsociety.co.uk/news/the-royal-british-legion-suspends-sales-of-its-offensive-rum.html

239 https://www.rt.com/uk/246369-oil-gas-falkland-islands/

240 https://www.falklands.gov.fk/self-sufficiency/the-islands-plan/#:~:text=Growth and diversification,are being implemented

the UK's economic outlook, but also with the fashionable, much vaunted World Economic Forum [241]global 'sustainability' model.

This late stage move to finite, dirty hydrocarbons keys in with [242]the surveys made in the years before the Argentine invasion, and Thatcher's written references to the strategic importance of the Falkland Islands:

> *'Thatcher wrote in her autobiography that 'the islands had obvious strategic importance', and during the Falklands war she attempted to win US support by emphasising their strategic role to President Reagan.'*

> **From *Britain and the Dictatorships of Argentina and Chile, 1973-82* by Grace Livingstone**

[243]Here's an excerpt [removed from the FIG website in December 2021, but retrieved using [244]the Wayback Machine] from the FIG's "Islands Plan" for the years '2014 to 2018 and beyond':

> *"We present this Islands Plan at an exciting time for the Falkland Islands. We are on the*

---

[241]   https://www.weforum.org/sustainability-world-economic-forum
[242]   https://api.parliament.uk/historic-hansard/written-answers/1982/apr/08/falkland-islands-2#:~:text=Mr. Onslow,a commercial basis.
[243]   https://www.falklands.gov.fk/assets/The-Islands-Plan-2014-2018-Compressed.pdf
[244]   http://web.archive.org/web/20211102192035/https:/www.falklands.gov.fk/assets/The-Islands-Plan-2014-2018-Compressed.pdf

> *cusp of potentially significant changes that a*
> *hydrocarbons industry may bring – but we*
> *must work hard to ensure that the desire for*
> *such an industry becomes a reality, and to*
> *ensure that the Islands are prepared to man-*
> *age its implications – on our economy, on our*
> *society and on our environment."*

The mobilisation of a task force 40 years ago, followed by the loss of hundreds of young lives, can't be seen as 'justified', given this screeching 2014 about-face by the FIG, with its lurch from natural farming to unnatural gas and oil.

This tiny outpost's frantic pursuit of difficult to exploit, un-sustainable fossil fuels risks jeopardising the UK population's support, which has been understandably wearing thin over the years. Thatcher's supposed justification for the conflict is now looking very shaky.

The islanders' aspirations seem to have shifted alarmingly. How can these newly announced wishes remain 'paramount' 40 years on? And how can British citizens – who continue to fund the islands' defence – continue to invest their money and trust into propping up the FIG?

Regardless of whether any oil or gas is ever brought to the surface, [245] it's envisaged the world's diminishing oil supplies will run out in 40 to 50 years anyway, and oil and gas in the Falkland Islands could only ever succeed as a stopgap.

---

[245] https://science.howstuffworks.com/environmental/energy/run-out-of-oil.htm#:~:text=How long is,of oil left.

Can [246]fishing and tourism alone – with exports [247]mainly to Spain and [248]imports mainly from the UK – sustain these islands in the long term? It seems unlikely. I'd describe the FIG's economic competence as myopic if not fatally flawed. Even if the oil and gas ventures are successful, they won't last, and there's a very real possibility the FIG will end up going on bended knee to the mother country for another large bailout in 40 years' time. Or perhaps a lot sooner.

[249]Rockhopper Exploration's Sealion Project still hasn't brought any oil to market. It would surprise nobody if the whole hydrocarbons idea was mothballed.

[250]In 2012 it was assumed that oil production would have taken off by 2018. We're still waiting for this to happen ten years on.

A future UK government may even become short on patience, hungry for trade and arms dealing opportunities and return to negotiating behind everyone's backs on sovereignty.

I hope this book provides some pause for thought.

＋＋＋＋＋＋

[246] https://en.wikipedia.org/wiki/Falkland_Islands
[247] https://en.wikipedia.org/wiki/Economy_of_the_Falkland_Islands#:~:text=Main export partners,US 4.9%25 (2004)
[248] https://en.wikipedia.org/wiki/Economy_of_the_Falkland_Islands#:~:text=Main import partners,France 3.6%25 (2004)
[249] https://en.mercopress.com/2020/08/18/falkland-islands-and-oil-companies-new-approach-to-stranded-assets#:~:text=The Sea Lion,unlikely to happen.
[250] https://en.mercopress.com/2012/10/26/falklands-to-build-a-new-deep-water-port-to-cater-for-the-oil-and-gas-industry

The small number of BBC links I've included are from a time before it dawned upon millions of us – a huge and growing international audience, hungry for objectivity – that the UK's national broadcaster, [251] post Savile, is no longer applying the journalistic standards and codes it once did as a matter of course. Judging by its highly polished, yet wayward news content, it appears to have 'taken the blue pill', [252] is now accepting donations from Bill Gates, has veered off course, and become one of the subservient, hugely influential propaganda arms of a [253] rapidly self-enriching, dominant global consensus.

All this meshes nicely with a manipulative UK establishment that regularly strongarms and hijacks the BBC's suspect operational output (who remembers the fake 'drift back to work' during the miners' strike?), whipping it into line and using its 'reporting' channels to wheel out calls for patriotism as a first resort, before softening us up for the next unwarranted, illegal military undertaking.

Unlike the current, completely unexplored, undebated coronavirus fear campaign, the press and media of the past 40 years has brought us some limited, not always balanced coverage of the pros and cons of military developments and ventures, even as

---

[251]   https://www.independent.co.uk/news/uk/politics/revealed-jimmy-sa-vile-s-close-friendship-with-margaret-thatcher-8432351.html

[252]   https://theduran.com/sars-cov-2-covid19-who-why-and-wtf/

[253]   https://www.dw.com/en/forbes-a-new-billionaire-every-17-hours/a-57135443#:~:text=With nearly 500 new billionaires in 2021%2C there,Bezos has a net worth of $177 billion

media audience figures and the captured, [254]billionaire-owned newspapers' sales have plummeted through the floor.

Notwithstanding the flag waving and rampant nationalism of the UK and Argentine press before, during and after the Falklands conflict, it eventually became clear – but too late – that there were 907 absolute imperatives for stating, "Never again", and for avoiding bloody conflicts like this in the future.

But as today's media commentators continue to trot out the same, tired old line; "Oh, we have to defend these islands or our boys will have died for nothing", and the hordes of men on the Clapham iPhone obediently parrot them, [255]it seems very few lessons were ever learned. The primary one being "Why didn't we inspect the peace plans that were on the table at the time, pause to take a breath, and avoid all that human carnage in the first place?"

With 20-22 hindsight, it appears the Falklands conflict may have been manipulated into position by political opportunists who deceitfully:

- ➤ *offered Falklands' sovereignty to Argentina*
- ➤ *forged trade deals on the sly*
- ➤ *sold arms to the junta*
- ➤ *slashed the UK's South Atlantic presence*

---

[254] https://en.wikipedia.org/wiki/Decline_of_newspapers#:~:text=United Kingdom%5Bedit,in 2009.%5B39%5D

[255] https://www.gov.uk/government/publications/human-augmentation-the-dawn-of-a-new-paradigm

> ➤ *encouraged an Argentine invasion*
> ➤ *pleaded to patriotism*
> ➤ *took an "Operation Corporate" gamble on their political fortunes*
> ➤ *won a war – and later an election – after recklessly placing our lives into the balance*

Meanwhile the fighting men on both sides of the conflict, including the author, had honestly and dutifully lined up as ready, obedient pawns, risking their own wellbeing and survival. But for what, exactly?

———————— ✦✦✦✦ ————————

Throughout this book, I've linked to many on the record political ambitions. These originated within successive, cross-party UK governments right back to the early 1960s, but primarily within the Conservative administration that held power between May 1979 and June 1983. I've linked to reports on what appears to be a dedicated, government-led snubbing of the interests of both the Falkland Islanders and the UK population, all in favour of runaway greed and political self-interest.

———————— ✦✦✦✦ ————————

Unlike a fellow Royal Navy Falklands veteran who now tells us he's no longer capable, I've sweated a lot in the creation of this book.

Tuesday 15th June

01:10 [256] Heard from the troops at Stanley (over the NGS circuit) "The surrender has been signed."

We are now in Berkeley Sound (North of Port Stanley) for an NGS as we still might be required. The weather is deteriorating. Getting quite rough now. We are not required for the NGS tonight.

17:00 Reports say that 15,000 enemy troops are being taken prisoner. This is much more than was estimated. The surrender should cover the whole South Atlantic, in the Falklands as well as at sea. Contrary to popular belief, the Argentinians were found to be well supplied. Arrangements are being made to evacuate them.

We have been told to proceed to South Georgia to meet up with the *[257]Endurance*, then proceed to the island of South Tule to evacuate 80 Argentinian soldiers and 30 Argentinian scientists (civilians). They have been on the island since 1976 (the scientists) and have ignored diplomatic pressure. We have been told to use minimum force if we have to remove them. We should arrive there on or around the 20th June. The *RFA Olmeda* is also with us and has an extra

---

256   https://www.nytimes.com/1982/06/17/world/text-of-surrender-document.html#:~:text=I,| Subscribe

257   http://www.solarnavigator.net/history/hms_endurance.htm

three months supplies for us in case we get stuck in the pack ice which surrounds the area. The Argentines on the island are reported to have either a Chinook helicopter or a C130 Hercules for ferrying supplies in and out.

The weather is very rough now. Our detachment from the main group has been delayed until the weather improves. Hopefully then we can get some mail onboard.

CONFIDENTIAL

THE LORD CHANCELLOR said that he was sure that he would be
speaking for every member of the Cabinet in offering congratulations to
the Prime Minister on the courage and clarity of purpose which she had
displayed throughout the crisis. The successful repossession of the
Falkland Islands reflected new lustre on British arms and engendered a
renewed sense of self-confidence in the British people.

THE PRIME MINISTER said that at 9.00 pm local time on 14 June the
British Land Forces Commander, Major General Moore, accepted from
the Argentine Commander in the Falkland Islands, General Menendez,
the surrender of all the Argentine armed forces in East and West
Falkland Islands together with their arms and equipment. Full
information about British casualties was not yet available but first
indications were that they had not been heavy in the final stages. Press
reports that General Menendez had left for Buenos Aires appeared to be
inaccurate. It was estimated that Argentine prisoners of war would
number some 15,000 of which 11,000 were in Port Stanley itself and
2,000 on West Falkland. The Argentines had little tentage and food for
three to four days only. British stocks of tents for prisoners had been
lost when the Atlantic Conveyor was sunk. For humanitarian reasons,
therefore, it would be necessary to repatriate most of the prisoners at
once. A message would be sent that day to the Argentine Government
to indicate that the British Government would be ready to repatriate the
prisoners to the nearest suitable port in Argentina using the British
ships, Canberra and Norland, provided that the Argentine Government
agreed that all hostilities between the two countries were at an end and
that safe conduct for the ships would be guaranteed. It was essential to
make certain that a comprehensive cessation of hostilities was achieved.
The Argentine Government would be told that, if they agreed to this, the
Government would lift the Total Exclusion Zone and other restrictions
and recommend to the other members of the European Community that
economic sanctions should be ended, as a first step towards the
restoration of normal relations. As an interim arrangement, as soon
as Port Stanley airfield could be reopened, Mr Rex Hunt would return,
with powers limited to those of civil administration; the responsibility
of Commander-in-Chief would be exercised by the British military
commander.

In discussion the point was made that, if the Argentine Government were reluctant to agree to a comprehensive cessation of hostilities it would be necessary to retain some Argentine prisoners of war; but conditions in the Islands were such that it would be necessary to repatriate the majority. There would be a strong demand to allow foreign journalists to visit the Islands. It would be helpful in terms of international opinion to agree to this; but conditions in the Islands might impose some delay. There would now be renewed demands on the Government to set up an inquiry into the events leading up to the Argentine invasion. It would be important for the inquiry to proceed expeditiously. Demands for an official inquiry into the Government's handling of the press during the operation should be resisted; but the Select Committee on Defence were likely to investigate the matter. The rightness of the decision to delay publication of the total number of casualties in the Argentine bombing raid on Bluff Cove had been demonstrated by the success of the operation against Port Stanley. By allowing the Argentine commander to believe that casualties had been much higher than they in fact were, and that the final British assault would in consequence be delayed, tactical surprise had been achieved and heavy British casualties in the final stages avoided. Press accusations that the intention to conduct operations against Darwin and Goose Green had been leaked in London were totally without foundation. There would now be international pressure on the United Kingdom to seek a diplomatic solution to the dispute with Argentina, in accordance with Resolution 502 of the United Nations Security Council. This would need to be handled firmly. That Resolution had been passed before British forces had been obliged, by Argentine failure to comply with it by a voluntary withdrawal, to repossess the Islands by force of arms.

THE PRIME MINISTER, summing up the discussion, said that the Cabinet would wish to offer their warm congratulations and grateful thanks to all those in the armed forces, the merchant marine and the civilian support services who had contributed to the outstanding success of the operation to repossess the Falkland Islands, and to mourn all those who had given their lives in the conflict. Consideration should now be given to the early publication of an official despatch on the operation. She would consult the Opposition Leaders about the Falkland Islands inquiry, which should not concentrate only on the events leading up to the invasion but should cover the whole background of negotiations with Argentina since 1965. It would not be appropriate for it to be a judicial inquiry. In accepting the Lord Chancellor's congratulations, she would wish to give credit to the Secretary of State for Defence and the other Ministers in day-to-day charge, who had enjoyed the full backing of the Cabinet and the British people in carrying out their policies.

The Cabinet -

1.   Warmly endorsed the Prime Minister's congratulations
to the armed forces, the merchant marine and the civilian
support services for the successful outcome of the operation
to recover the Falkland Islands.

2.   Noted that the Prime Minister would now consult
the Opposition Leaders with a view to proceeding as
expeditiously as possible with the proposed Falkland
Islands inquiry.

3.   Invited the Secretary of State for Defence to examine
the possibility of early publication of an official despatch
on the operation.

Cabinet Office

15 June 1982

2
CONFIDENTIAL

Wednesday 16th June

There is rioting in Buenos Aires. The Argentine public seem to be unhappy about the way Galtieri has handled the conflict and they are calling for a new government. They also want the troops back on the Falklands and fighting again, according to the news reports. Galtieri has said he will not give up fighting for the Malvinas.

Reports of Argentinian stocks of dum-dum bullets found. They explode on contact.

Argentinian police used tear gas and batons to control the rioting crowds in Buenos Aires.

Task force Commander is pressing Galtieri for an answer to his request for an end to military action. He has said a lot of Argentinians are suffering various illnesses associated with the bad weather and we are unable to look after them properly whilst still under threat from the remainder of the Argentinian armed forces.

We have R/V'd with *HMS Brilliant,* and we now have mail and newspapers onboard.

Thursday 17th June

The weather has improved a great deal and we are on our way to South Georgia in company with *Olmeda*. *Endurance* has already sailed for

South Thule. We should arrive at South Georgia on the 18th June. More mail for us on *HMS Dumbarton Castle.*

The Argentine Junta and top-ranking military officials are said to be divided over whether to end hostilities or resume negotiations. 12 out of 14 were for negotiations. Galtieri is reported to have absolved himself of any responsibility for the surrender and the ex-Falklands based commander Menendez is receiving the blame. [258] *5,000 Argentine troops are now onboard the cruise-liner Canberra* for repatriation via Uruguay. Argentine Junta won't allow them back in through Argentine ports.

HMS Glamorgan has left for home.

Welsh Guards who survived the bombing attack on *RFA Sir Galahad* have arrived back in the UK from Montevideo.

HMS Arrow has left for home.

19:30 News just came in that Galtieri is to be removed from his position as president and overall commander of the armed forces. A General Nikolaites is said to be taking over temporarily.

---

[258] https://www.nam.ac.uk/explore/british-army-and-falklands-war#:~:text=repatriating argentine prisoners of war (pows) was a long process. some 5%2C000 prisoners were embarked on 'canberra' and 1%2C000 on 'norland' on 17 june. by 20 june%2C 10%2C250 prisoners had been repatriated.

He is said to be a hard-liner against hostilities being ceased. But he might only be in power whilst the reshuffle is taking place.

Canberra and *Norland* are going straight into Argentina rather than via Uruguay as this will get the injured back in quicker. Argentina using some of their own ships as well.

Friday 18th June

Latest Junta communique says Argentina will only end hostilities when all British troops are pulled out, the blockade is ended, [259]*and EEC sanctions are finished.*

The first load of Argentine prisoners are on their way home direct to Argentina. Britain are retaining 1,000 senior officers and commanders until the guarantee of the cessation of hostilities is received.

We stopped off at South Georgia today. [260]*A very impressive sight.* Mountainous. A few small icebergs here and there.

In line with President Reagan urging Thatcher to work for a peaceful conclusion to the conflict, [261]a sympathetic New York

---

[259] https://www.jstor.org/stable/40395502?seq=1

[260] https://www.youtube.com/watch?v=0O57R7iLdpM

[261] https://www.nytimes.com/1982/06/18/world/galteiri-resigns-argentina-new-leaders-say-they-d-bring-pow-s-home-with-british.html

Times article from today claims that right-wing dictator, US ally and Dirty War collaborator General Galtieri 'resigned' and wasn't forced out.

⁺⁺✦✦✦⁺⁺

Saturday 19ᵗʰ June

²⁶²*Now on our way to South Thule.* Weather okay.

HMS Plymouth has left for home.

Endurance landed troops on the island of South Thule. Argentines issued a communique saying that this was in direct contradiction of the UN calling for an end to hostilities in the South Atlantic. They say that helicopters flew in firing machine guns. UK Ministry of Defence haven't released any statement.

HMS Glasgow arrived back in Portsmouth today.

Sunday 20ᵗʰ June

Still on our way to South Thule. Should arrive there today sometime. *12:00* At South Thule, ready to do NGS if required. It's snowing upstairs.

12:25 Ten personnel coming down towards our landing party, waving white flag. Looks like they've surrendered on South Thule. The island

---

²⁶² https://en.wikipedia.org/wiki/Operation_Keyhole

is being searched for anyone else. Ship closing to one mile. Hands back to defence watches.

Monday 21st June

01:00 Argentines still undecided about a new president.

[263] *The Argentine Air Force* say they will split from the Junta if a civilian or their commander Lami Doso is not chosen. Britain have issued statement about South Thule being recaptured and 11 scientists found.

14:00 We're leaving the area now to head back for the Falklands. The prisoners will be moved onboard here and offloaded when we reach the Falklands.

Tuesday 22nd June

05:00 Still no announcement yet of a new Argentine president. Argentine Air Force still threatening to leave the Junta if the Army's nominee is approved.

---

263 https://www.nytimes.com/1982/06/17/world/argentine-junta-ago-nizes-over-its-response-to-british.html#:~:text=the divisions were reflected politically as well. the air force has called for president galtieri to step down as president and for the junta as a whole to take over more of the daily decisions of government. it has offered to put up brigadier lami dozo as chairman of the junta

On our way back to the Falklands via South Georgia. On arrival at Grytviken (S. Georgia) we will take on the prisoners and *Olmeda* will proceed back to the UK.

19:00 [264]*The Argentine military Junta has collapsed.* The Air Force and the Navy broke away and the Army is planning to run the political side on its own. A General Bignone is taking over, and he has said Argentina will have a democracy by 1984. The three services will only operate together in military affairs.

20:00 We are still on our way to South Georgia (about 120 miles southeast).

Wednesday 23rd June

11:00 Back at South Georgia. Picking up prisoners. 11 prisoners are in one of the dining halls.

---

[264] https://www.nytimes.com/1982/06/22/world/argentine-junta-appears-at-odds.html#:~:text=a spokesman for the air force said its high command had threatened not to support a government with an army man at its head%2C in what appeared to be a growing rift within the military junta.

Thursday 24ᵗʰ June

On our way back to the Falklands.

16:00 Still proceeding back. ETA 25ᵗʰ at approx. 15:00.

Three British journalists held in Argentina are to be released on bail. Argentina are reported to have said they were going to invade the Falklands this month but took advantage of the scrap merchants landing on South Georgia first.

Friday 25ᵗʰ June

ETA at Port Stanley is now 12:00.

12:15 Arrived Port Stanley, prisoners dropped off ashore. Mail taken onboard.

18:00 Detached again to join up with the *Hermes* group.

Saturday 26ᵗʰ June

Back with the *Hermes* group in the TEZ. More mail and newspapers taken onboard.

23:00 Possible Super Etendard detected heading east.

AIR RAID WARNING YELLOW

Sunday 27th June

A/C must have turned around but don't know any info as yet.

08:00 Nothing further on any A/C received.

21:11 Possible Hercules sighted near Argentine coast, heading east. There has been increased Argentine air activity throughout today, though reason unclear. Maybe a possible special forces drop over the Falklands?

Monday 28th June

16:00 Reports from Buenos Aires say that Argentina are now ready to accept a full end to hostilities and the Argentines are going to accept Resolution 502. News comes from a Buenos Aires newspaper.

17:00 Our captain has been recommended for a DSC after *HMS Yarmouth*'s courageous actions in San Carlos water and the *Ardent* incident. *Hermes* and *Broadsword* are going back on the 3rd or 4th July. No mention of *Yarmouth* going back yet. *Fearless* and *Intrepid* are on their way back.

Tuesday 29ᵗʰ June

12:00 The Argentine foreign ministry say they have no knowledge of any message being sent to the UN. An Argentine newspaper said a message had been sent to the UN saying Argentina will now comply with Resolution 502.

Wednesday 30ᵗʰ June

Nothing much happening. Still with *Hermes* group

Thursday 1ˢᵗ July

We've been detached to meet with *British Enterprise III* who has a major engine defect and no power. Either us or the tug *Typhoon* will be towing her south. Argentina have sworn in a new president, [265]*ex-General Bignone* (for an interim period).

---

[265] https://www.seattletimes.com/seattle-news/obituaries/reynaldo-big-none-last-leader-of-argentinas-murderous-dictatorship-dies-at-90/

LRO Paul

Friday 2ⁿᵈ July to Sunday 4ᵗʰ July

QUIET. NOT MUCH HAPPENING. More mail onboard.

²⁶⁶*Lord Chalfont obituary – By the Falkland Islands Association*

Monday 5ᵗʰ July

Signal received telling us to proceed back to Ascension Island / UK on the 7ᵗʰ July. Reckon we'll be escorting the *MV St Edmund*. Argentina have still not said whether hostilities in the South Atlantic are over.

---

²⁶⁶ https://www.fiassociation.com/article/1522/lord_chalfont_obe__
mc__pc#:~:text=ear.-,The UK had%2C,of the Falkland Islanders.,-Forewarned

Tuesday 6ᵗʰ July

90ᵗʰ day at sea today.

Wednesday 7ᵗʰ July

_15:00_ We're not turning north and are on our way back to UK via Ascension Island. We should be at Ascension Island by 17ᵗʰ July. Then it will take us till 30ᵗʰ July to get back to Rosyth.

RO Cameron, LRO Frank, LRO Paul

8ᵗʰ July to Saturday 10ᵗʰ July

Quiet. Still on our way back with *Exeter* and *Cardiff*.

Sunday 11ᵗʰ July

We've been told we may get back in Rosyth on the morning of the 28ᵗʰ July.

Monday 12ᵗʰ July

Still heading toward Ascension. ETA now 16ᵗʰ July in the evening. 96ᵗʰ day at sea.

[267]*THE END*

"World conquest is believed in most firmly by those who know it to be impossible" –

[268]*George Orwell*

---

[267] https://www.youtube.com/watch?v=FPm79YGIiyc

[268] https://quotefancy.com/quote/1904635/George-Orwell-World-con-quest-is-believed-in-most-firmly-by-those-who-know-it-to-be

I briefly referred earlier to some broken humans who needed dealing with. These were local council directors – my employers – who tried to sack me, but without any justification.

Letter to council directors, sent during workplace dispute:

Hello All,   11th November 2008

26 years ago, I served onboard HMS Yarmouth during the Falklands conflict. During this period, I was involved in rescuing survivors from HMS Sheffield, HMS Ardent and stood by ready to take survivors off HMS Glamorgan if called upon. These were my work colleagues at the time and I will never forget the relief on their faces, the tragic events and those who were injured or died.

Fast forward to 2008 and I'm sad to report shameful treatment by certain managers. I don't intend to let this situation break me, but want it to be known that I'm currently suffering quite badly as a result of foul and inappropriate behaviour.

Despite all this, I'll continue to keep my head held high and focus on my past experiences, my wife and lovely kids, the future and the wider world beyond here. I vow not to let selfish and cowardly individuals destroy me and my family.

It would not be fair to name these people, because already they have to live with themselves and the consequences of their ruthless actions.

Thanks for your time and thank you to those truly brave work colleagues who have stood firm and supported me,

Paul Cardin
Engineering Assistant

[269]*In September 2019, I celebrated 10 years out of the rat race. For two and a half years, I'd been bullied and gaslit by my council employer. This photo is from my 50th birthday - just before my final disciplinary hearing. Under threat of dismissal,* [270]*I was forced to defend myself, my wife, my children, and my former work colleagues.*

[269] https://wirralinittogether.blog/2019/09/06/this-week-we-are-celebrating-10-years-out-of-the-rat-race/

[270] https://www.youtube.com/watch?v=BOPRg0C8dSM

CHAPTER

This may look like a departure from the subject matter, but it's worth including because UK and US militaries have a growing, but largely unseen influence here.

When I left the Royal Navy 40 years ago, it coincided with the advent of the home computer, which was a perfectly timed development for me. Personal computers fascinated me, drew me in, and I also had the analytical and keyboard skills to carry forward into this new hi-tech area.

In the early 1990s, the arrival of public internet access offered those who could afford it some great opportunities. Or so we thought. On the surface, it was the dawn of a promising, new utopia and a chance to empower ourselves as citizens.

But beneath the surface, this gradually began to slip away, due to [271] the security services' paranoia, surveillance and inva-

---

[271] https://www.theguardian.com/world/2013/sep/05/nsa-gchq-encryp-tion-codes-security

sions of our privacy, the creeping domination of Silicon Valley, the [272] rancid conduct of social media companies, and the [273] on-going failure by governments to properly regulate their friends, the corporate abusers. And thanks to [274] those actively seeking / imposing behavioural change, it's now descending into a threatening, new dystopia.

Ultimately, despite the early promise, we never got to a position where we could reach across national boundaries, come together and safely help each other to make progress online. Wedges have been driven between people, suspicion and hatred have been encouraged and there's been little sense of togetherness or any sign of a building and growing online community even after all this time.

A wonderful opportunity has been squandered and the position taken up by governments and the big social media players still appears to be a distant and defensive one: you're either with us or you're against us. Say the wrong thing and you're suspended until you comply, and if not, you're banned.

Most dignified citizens, capable of critical thinking, would not risk blind compliance or the surrender of their trust across to billionaire tech oligarchs, toxic corporations, defence departments and military and secret service spy networks who are all in league, and continue to prosper, whilst colluding to wrest

---

[272] https://theintercept.com/2020/10/15/facebook-and-twitter-cross-a-line-far-more-dangerous-than-what-they-censor/

[273] https://www.bbc.co.uk/news/technology-55318225

[274] https://www.wired.co.uk/article/inside-the-77th-brigade-britains-information-warfare-military

control, re-shape the internet to their own ends, and destroy it for the user.

The original promise of safe, secure, unimpeded access – [275] *even though the web was military in origin and therefore fundamentally stillborn – may have brought some unintended benefits. But it feels like we're now being carefully drip-fed our information privileges when it suits them.*

That said, despite the ongoing, routine surveillance and stockpiling of our private and personal data, the growing censorship, the more recent influx of powerful corporate interests and the neutering of most of the independent content, if we know the ropes, the web still offers us a convenient and accessible pathway to precious information.

Finding worthwhile independent news content, [276] *despite the meddling and anti-trust conduct of Google and others, has generally become easier if you know where to look.*

But ensuring your views get heard – particularly on social media – not so much.

For me, it's been frustrating at times, but it's also been [277] *fascinating, educational and highly productive. Above all, it's never been time wasted.*

---

[275] https://www.rooshv.com/the-internet-was-created-as-a-surveillance-network

[276] https://www.vox.com/2017/6/27/15878980/europe-fine-google-anti-trust-search

[277] https://youtu.be/2BX55_Ddp-k?t=1284

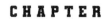

Finally, a few pointed questions…

How did the Falklands conflict come about?

Did Thatcher slash the islands' defence cover and enter sovereignty talks in a planned, calculated manner, to trigger an Argentine invasion?

Or was the Argentine invasion jointly and secretly conceived, precipitated, and manoeuvred into place?

Why did most of the UK population place their trust in the sudden flag-waving and tub-thumping of a UK government that right up until the invasion had been privately selling arms to the junta and was keen to do a deal, and have the islands' sovereignty passed across to Argentina?

We have an answer to this last question; millions of voters knew nothing of their government's duplicity. They'd been cleverly led up the garden path. When a large majority voted Tory in June 1983, they'd been successfully gaslit by the rejoicing media, and were completely oblivious of Thatcher's clandestine arms dealing, and the trade and sovereignty approaches to the Argentine junta. But by then it was too late, the dirty deeds had been done. To protect the guilty, the full details were swiftly concealed and embargoed under the [278] '30-year rule' until the year 2012. Some of it for 40 years longer, when most veterans and contemporary journalists and historians will be dead.

Behind our backs, Thatcher had been trying to secure secret deals with a right-wing junta. One that had spent many years torturing and [279] disappearing tens of thousands of its own law-abiding citizens. [280] She was also trying to secure arms deals with the Argentine junta, right up until four days before the invasion.

40, 50, 60 years on, it's likely many of the missing people were murdered by death squads, and now occupy shallow, unmarked graves. They'll never be seen or heard from again. Thatcher quite carefully chose to stay mute and to not criticise or embarrass the rogue governments of the United States, Argentina, Chile, Uruguay and Brazil for their prolonged involvement in these extra-judicial atrocities.

We've travelled a long way since 1982. Most of it has been spent careering in the wrong direction. Are the [281] Five Eyes

---

[278] https://en.wikipedia.org/wiki/Thirty-year_rule

[279] https://www.bbc.co.uk/news/world-latin-america-48632231

[280] https://declassifieduk.org/margaret-thatchers-secret-deal-ings-with-the-argentine-military-junta-that-invaded-the-falk-lands/#:~:text=Viewing arms exports,regime bomber airplanes.

[281] https://en.wikipedia.org/wiki/Five_Eyes

nations and several nodding dog EU states keeping their back yards safe, as claimed, or is their behaviour making the rest of the world unsafe?

I would suggest the latter.

What kind of a world is it where welcome outbreaks of peace get translated by default into direct affronts to the war interests of governments, corporations, media, and arms manufacturers, who react by agitating further, sowing uncertainty, heightening fear, and restoring us all back to a kneejerk war footing?

What kind of a world is it where the 1982 invasion of some distant, largely unknown islands can cause outrage within the UK establishment, gain assistance from the USA in their recovery and result in 907 deaths? Particularly after [282] the 1965 invasion and theft of the Chagos Islands from Mauritius by the same UK establishment – again, assisted by the USA. Almost six decades later, the Falklands issue is resolved, but the Chagos Islands people and their descendants are still awaiting repatriation.

In May 2019, [283] Sir Roger Carr, Chairman of the world's fourth largest arms manufacturer, BAE Systems, was covertly recorded speaking to his shareholders:

"Civilians are killed in war. The solution is to stop wars at the earliest opportunity. And our belief is that if you supply first

---

[282]   https://www.theguardian.com/world/2021/jun/03/the-chagos-is-lands-a-millstone-around-the-neck-of-british-diplomacy

[283]   https://electronicintifada.net/content/weapons-trade-saudis-and-isra-el-must-be-disrupted/34191

class equipment, you are the encouragement, particularly when used in defence, for people to stop fighting."

Carr's company has channelled billions of pounds worth of weapons to the Saudi Arabian hereditary dictatorship via Cyprus. The Saudis are routinely targeting civilians in Yemen after invading the country in 2015. Seven years later, they're still there and still dropping bombs.

A nationwide famine has started, and continues, but the killing hasn't stopped. So, it seems Carr is eager to provide munitions which are used to endlessly bomb civilians 'back into peace', make a lot of money doing that, keep many of the people of Lancashire, UK, in the lifestyles to which they've become accustomed, and help to starve those Yemenis left alive on behalf of his investors.

Increasingly, more innocent lives are coming under threat the world over. The Falklands conflict was brief, took place a long way away, and pales into insignificance alongside the deliberate, unprovoked, 'endless war' events of today.

We should research, educate ourselves, unite to expose the eugenicist strategies at the top level, remove our consent, our tacit approval, and demand positive action on the world stage. We're poorly served by failed governments, many of whom — under the guise of 'defence' — are expanding militarily, agitating overseas, [284]giving absolute free rein to their own secret

---

[284] https://www.yorkshireeveningpost.co.uk/read-this/mi5-agents-are-legally-allowed-to-commit-torture-and-murder-in-the-uk-in-the-line-of-duty-3161395

services, [285] *ingratiating themselves with and arming oppressive middle east dictatorships, torturing captives, and continuing to send you or your offspring to their deaths on a lie. All without an ounce of compassion for their victims.*

The time is now. Despite the threatened clampdowns, mandatory medical interventions, and growing censorship, if you're online with a laptop, desktop computer, tablet, or mobile phone, you have some of the means at your disposal. War isn't Peace. Freedom isn't Slavery. Ignorance isn't Strength, but Knowledge **is** *Power.*

And not just via technology. Let's wake up, enlighten ourselves, stop acquiescing, realise where the actual power lies, shake off our chains, get out there on the streets in our reasonable, tranquil, determined millions and hold these dangerous psychopaths' feet to the fire. They fear us because they know that we, the largely sleeping masses, hold that power and could wield it to re-align the world and establish our dominance.

If only we knew it.

Hopefully, showing such disrespect won't get me blackballed by the local country club.

Paul Cardin, January 2022.

---

[285] https://declassifieduk.org/britain-backs-most-of-the-worlds-repressive-regimes-new-analysis-shows

Lightning Source UK Ltd.
Milton Keynes UK
UKHW031305031122
411585UK00006B/121